GUIDE TO BOOKS ON LITERACY

THE NATIONAL LITERACY TRUST'S INTERNATIONAL ANNOTATED BIBLIOGRAPHY 1999

Julia Davies and Jo Weinberger

Trentham Books

Stoke on Trent, UK and Sterling, USA

Trentham Books Limited

Westview House	22883 Quicksilver Drive
734 London Road	Sterling
Oakhill	VA 20166-2012
Stoke on Trent	USA
Staffordshire	
England ST4 5NP	

First published 2000

British Library Cataloguing-in-Publication Data
A catalogue record for this book is available from the British Library

1 85856 234 1 (paperback)

Designed and typeset by Trentham Print Design Ltd., Chester and printed in Great Britain by Cromwell Press Ltd., Wiltshire.

GUIDE TO BOOKS ON LITERACY

THE NATIONAL LITERACY TRUST'S INTERNATIONAL ANNOTATED BIBLIOGRAPHY 1999

Contents

The National Literacy Trust's Guide to Books on Literacy 1999

Books continue to be published on many and diverse topics within the field of literacy, and it has been stimulating to explore the range of new publications which have come out in the last year. Our continuing interest in all dimensions of literacy motivates us in the task of compiling this bibliography. It requires scrutiny of all relevant sources of information about new books relating to literacy, including publishers' catalogues, the *British National Bibliography* (BNB), the World Wide Web and personal recommendations. What has been apparent is that books on literacy have increasingly been viewed as having common features and are more often listed together – although as many books are classified under psychology, media studies, linguistics and other subject disciplines. Listing all these various publications between one set of covers offers readers the means to trace all new publications in their particular area of literacy, and the chance to browse and discover developments in the field.

Our philosophy for including books
We have kept a similar format to the previous lists, to ensure continuity and allow for comparisons across editions. However, this edition reveals one major change: the National Literacy Strategy has provided a major focus for recent literacy publications in the UK market. A few words of explanation are perhaps needed for readers outside England. The National Literacy Strategy is a major government initiative, begun in English primary schools at the beginning of the school year (autumn) 1998. It is based largely on the practice developed in the preceding National Literacy Project (DfEE, 1997). The National Literacy Strategy represents an unprecedented intervention in classroom teaching methods, being the first

England-wide policy on the teaching of reading. The NLS was not implemented through an act of parliament, yet English schools are anticipated to adopt it; schools which opt out are expected to do so in close consultation with their local education authority. Distinctive features of the NLS that are often referred to in the literature about it, are a daily Literacy Hour, with components of whole text, sentence and word level work, that are informed by teaching objectives set out in a national Literacy Strategy Framework for teaching (DfEE, 1998). More information about the hour can be gained from the National Literacy Trust at

http://www.literacytrust.org.uk/Database/index.html

This brief explanation may help to contextualise the wide range of publications this year which mention the Literacy Strategy or Literacy Hour. As a result of this government initiative, as well as reflecting many publishers' current priorities, recent books on literacy are often highly practical, with a 'how to do it' orientation. Those based on research findings have been listed here, while others, often compilations of photocopiable materials, were not thought appropriate to include in a guide to the publications exploring the underlying nature of literacy.

We have also noticed an increase in the number of books this year which regard Information and Communications Technology texts as a dimension of literacy. It is argued that ICT has facilitated new ways of writing, given rise to new types of text, and generated unique ways of reading which differ from the experience offered by conventional texts. This has implications for teaching and research and we have included books which address these topics and also those which attempt to deconstruct the WWW reading process and which guide readers in accessing new literacies.

We have again looked to *Reading Today* (Cassidy and Cassidy, 1999/2000) to see which issues were rated by leading literacy specialists as 'hot'. Guided reading was rated very hot indeed, and new topics rated hot were research-based practice, standards for reading and teacher education for reading. Phonemic awareness and volunteer tutoring were less hot topics than last year. This is a trend more clearly reflected in research articles than books, but it is interesting to note how dynamic the field is, with ever-changing emphases and priorities, some driven by practice and some by policy and external demands. This is particularly evident in the number of UK publications relating to the National Literacy Strategy.

We have reproduced a table that we featured in last year's Bibliography (Finlay and Weinberger, 1999), highlighting trends in literacy books over the years 1998-1999. This needs to be treated with some caution because although we have aimed to be as comprehensive as possible, there are inevitably omissions. However, changes to note are fewer books on writing and assessment in 1999 but more on special educational needs (here the influence of the National Literacy Strategy shows itself). Interestingly, however, overall proportions of other books in the different categories of literacy remain relatively constant.

Percentage distribution and rank order across all literacy categories in the 1998 and 1999 Bibliographies

Category	1998	1999	% change	Change in rank
Literacy in the early and primary years	20%	20%	no change	no change
Perspectives on literacy	14%	17%	+3%	no change
Focus on writing	14%	7%	-7%	-3
Focus on reading	12%	10%	-2%	no change
Focus on language	10%	5%	-5%	-2
Literacy for young adults and adults	7%	4%	-3%	-2
Focus on special needs	6%	10%	+4%	+3
Reference books	6%	7%	+1%	+1
Focus on libraries	4%	5%	+1%	+1
Focus on assessment	4%	2%	-2%	-3
Focus on family literacy	2%	5%	+3%	no change
Literacy in the secondary years	2%	8%	+6%	+2

We would like to mention that occasionally relevant books are inadvertently overlooked, so, as in earlier editions of the NLT Bibliography, we have included a few books from last year which had been previously omitted.

Practical Points

We have kept to the arrangements for entries used in previous editions, with the author's name followed by the title, followed by the number of pages, place of publication and publisher, hardback and paperback ISBN numbers. We have tried to be as comprehensive as possible in the entries given, and have provided addresses for publications which might otherwise be difficult to locate.

Intended Readership

We anticipate that the *Guide* will be of interest to undergraduates and postgraduates, teachers across the age range, adult basic skills tutors, university and college lecturers, literacy consultants, researchers, librarians, parents and all those concerned with what literacy is, what uses it has and the nature of its effects.

References:

Cassidy, Jack and Cassidy, Drew (1999/2000) What's Hot, What's Not for 2000. *Reading Today* December 1999/January 2000, Vol. 17, No. 3, p1, p28.

DfEE (1997) *The Implementation of the National Literacy Strategy.* London: Department for Education and Employment.

DfEE (1998) *National Literacy Strategy Framework.* London: Department for Education and Employment.

Finlay, Ann and Weinberger, Jo (1999) *The National Literacy Trust's International Annotated Bibliography of Books on Literacy.* Stoke on Trent: Trentham Books.

This years' entries in the bibliography have been written by Julia Davies and Jo Weinberger, with the assistance of other members of the Literacy@Sheffield research group: Ann Finlay, Peter Hannon, Jackie Marsh, Elaine Millard and Cathy Nutbrown. We are very grateful to Lorraine Roe for her secretarial assistance, and to Denise Harrison, at Sheffield University library, for her continuing support.

[The views contained are those of the compilers, and not necessarily those of the National Literacy Trust].

Julia Davies and Jo Weinberger, April 2000

BOOKS ON LITERACY

Perspectives on Literacy

Aikman, Sheila *Intercultural Education and Literacy: an Ethnographic Study of Indigenous Knowledge and Learning in the Peruvian Amazon. Studies in Written Language and Literacy 7*, 231pp. Amsterdam and Philadelphia: John Benjamins Publishing Company. ISBN: hbk 90272 1800 5 (Eur.) 1 55619 385 8 (US).

Cultural pluralism has been gaining recognition over the past decade, with the increasing development of approaches to education for indigenous peoples that acknowledge the intercultural nature of their lives. This book examines an ethnographic case study of the learning processes of the Arakmbut people of San Jose, in the Peruvian Amazon. Their oral culture and the proposed introduction of a biliterate schooled model of learning are examined, exploring to what extent such an educational model can promote indigenous learning processes and a sense of cultural identity. From the 1950s, teaching in the area had been delivered by Spanish speaking missionaries, but in the 1990s, indigenous organisations began working towards intercultural education. However, the Arakmbut in the study have been sceptical about bilingual education and question whether school is well placed to teach their language or way of life, whilst recognising that it does give them access to literacy in the national language of Spanish. The study explores within a methodological, political and historical context the interests, cultural practices and informal learning of the Arakmbut community of San Jose, examining the nature of education for and by indigenous peoples. This is a scholarly book, with extensive references.

Alvermann, Donna E, Moon, Jennifer S and Hagood, Margaret C *Popular Culture in the Classroom: Teaching and Researching Critical Media Literacy* 158pp. Delaware USA International Reading Association Illinois National Reading Conference. ISBN: pbk.0872072452. *Available from the International Reading Association, 800 Barksdale Road, Po Box 8139, Newark, Delaware 19714-8139, USA.*

This provocatively written text asserts that a broad range of popular culture texts are appropriate for classroom study, including computer games, the Internet and music. The authors explain the term 'critical media literacy' and offer detailed descriptions of teaching experiences, working across the age range with media texts. Critical media literacy teaching is strongly justified through careful argument and well documented examples of classroom work. The study demonstrates the need to teach a critical awareness of texts while showing sensitivity towards the texts themselves, which are often of real importance to young people. This research based study is an important contribution to debates seeking to define the literacy curriculum and is directed towards teachers, researchers and all those interested in literacy, popular culture, the media and teaching.

Barton, David, Hamilton, Mary and Ivanič, Roz *Situated Literacies: Reading and Writing in Context* 222pp. London and New York: Routledge. ISBN: pbk 0 415 20671 5.

With an illuminating foreword by Denny Taylor from the US, this interesting collection of chapters outlines current issues in literacy from the perspective of the New Literacy Studies. It is written by a group of academics from Lancaster University UK, with invited contributors working in a similar vein: James Paul Gee from the US, Janet Maybin from the UK and Renata de Pourbaix from Canada. Topics include using photographs to explore literacy practice, literacy in prisons, literacy in agriculture, children's project work, family literacy, literacy in an electronic community, literacy work with students, plus a number of chapters which explore aspects of the characteristics of literacy. Links are made throughout between specific contexts, studied from an ethnographic point of view, and social practices concerning literacy in a broader sense. An accessible and lively text, fully supported by references at the end of each chapter, this is a useful book for all those involved in literacy education, and anyone interested in current research and the development of new ideas in literacy theory and practice.

Burke, Jim *I Hear America Reading: Why We Read*, What We Read 116pp. Portsmouth NH: Heinemann. ISBN: pbk 0 325 00134 0. *Available in the UK through The Eurospan Group, 3, Henrietta Street, Covent Garden, London WC2E 8LU, UK.*

This is a highly engaging collection of letters responding to the author's open invitation to newspaper readers to share their stories of reading with his class of somewhat reluctant readers. Burke received over four hundred letters from young and old, from the well educated and the very young and barely literate. The letters testify to the value of reading, often offering detailed descriptions of epiphanous moments in a correspondent's reading experiences. The collection offers insight into the range of reasons for reading and the role reading plays in different people's lives. This is a fascinating collection and would serve as an interesting resource for teachers, a rich piece of data for researchers and a treasure trove of quotations for all those with a use for inspiring soundbytes!

Cox, Brian (Ed.) *Literacy is Not Enough: Essays on the Importance of Reading* 175pp. Manchester: Manchester University Press. ISBN: pbk 0 7190 5669 1. (1998).

In his introduction to this edited collection, Cox reminds his readers of a fundamental principle enshrined in The Cox Report (DES 1989) that a National Curriculum for English should embrace both the 'unity and diversity' of our multicultural society. This involves respect for diversity as well as an understanding of 'English inheritance'. The common view which the twenty different contributors to this volume share, is that 'Literacy is not Enough', but that critical literacy should be embraced by teachers of English. This is a collection of provocative essays from academics, teachers and politicians who variously discuss English teaching and assessment. They look, for example, at the affects of assessment on the teaching of reading; the influence of television and popular culture and the gradual erosion, by recent curriculum initiatives, of values previously set out in *The Cox Report* (DES 1989). This text will be of interest to all those involved in literacy, culture and education.

Reference: DES and the Welsh Office (1989) *English for Ages 5-16* (The Cox Report) London: HMSO.

Durgunoğlu, Aydin, Y and Verhoeven, Ludo (Eds.) *Literacy Development in a Multilingual Context: Cross-Cultural Perspectives* 303pp. Mahwah, New Jersey and London: Lawrence Erlbaum Associates. ISBN: pbk 0 8058 2443 X. *Available in the UK through The Eurospan Group, 3, Henrietta Street, Covent Garden, London WC2E 8LU, UK.*

The editors have collected together fourteen research papers, each well referenced and with common author and subject indexes at the end of the book. The book is aimed at an academic audience although it may also interest literacy teachers working in multilingual contexts. The papers explore the use and development of literacy in a variety of sociolinguistic situations. An anthropological perspective, dealing with the individual and society, is taken in Part 1. Cross-cultural perspectives covered in Part 1 include Gujerati speakers in England and Cambodian speakers in the USA. Part 2 discusses issues from a psychological perspective and the development of the individual. Bilingual examples include becoming English-Hebrew biliterate in Canada, and linguistic training for minorities in Norway. Issues in Part 3 are dealt with from an educational perspective and individual development and examples here range from literacy for girls in rural Pakistan to literacy education in Putonghua (Mandarin) for speakers of Chinese dialects.

Dusinberre, Juliet *Alice to the Lighthouse: Children's Books and Radical Experiments in Art* (first published 1987, reissued with alterations) 352pp. Basingstoke: Macmillan Press. In the United States Saint Martin's Press. ISBN: hbk 0 333 75984 2. ISBN: pbk 0 333 65850 7.

This re-issued version of *Alice to the Lighthouse* keeps alive the author's project to 'demonstrate the symbiotic relation between children's books and adult writing and the close connections between the ways in which a society views children and the books it produces for them to read' (p. xv). The book draws richly on quotations and illustrations from children's literature of the latter half of the 19th century. The opening chapter 'Children's Books, Childhood and Modernism' sets the tone of the book and alerts readers to the themes which are given deeper treatment in subsequent chapters. Chapter titles are enticing – and do not disappoint: The Voice of the Author; Virginia Woolf and the Irreverent Garden; Death; the Medium of Art; Making Space for a Child; The Literary and the Literal. This is a scholarly work and thoroughly sourced. It offers much to those interested in children's literature of the 19th century and in the process can inspire thinking about modern children's literature of the late 20th and early 21st centuries. For as Dusinberre illustrates throughout:

'The absence of a deliberately pointed moral, and of linear direction in narrative, the abdication of the author as preacher, and the use of words as play, all of which were pioneered in children's books in the later half of the nineteenth century, fed into the work of Virginia Woolf and her generation of writers. *Alice to the Lighthouse* charts the passage of a whole culture from *Alice's Adventures in Wonderland* and *Through the looking Glass* through Freud and Froebel, Sully and Roger Fry, towards Virginia Woolf's *To the Lighthouse.*'

This is a source of reference for those interested in the meanings which can be made from and through children's literature.

Gambrell, Linda B, Mandell Morrow, Lesley, Neuman, Susan B and Pressley, Michael (Eds.) *Best Practices in Literacy Instruction* 336pp. London and New York: The Guildford Press. ISBN: pbk 1 572 30443X. Available from 72, Spring Street, New York, NY 100012 USA.

This collection, emanating from research and experience in the United States, is contextualised within an educational climate of national level reform for raising levels of literacy. It is divided into three main sections: 'Perspectives on Exemplary Practices in Literacy', 'Strategies for Learning and Teaching' and 'Special Issues'. The first addresses fundamental principles in literacy teaching, arguing for resistance to prescriptive practices and the need to balance student and curricular needs. The second and largest section describes a range of practices in literacy development, drawing on classroom research. Each chapter examines a different aspect of literacy teaching, ranging from comprehension strategies to writing processes and interpretation. Finally, the 'Special Issues' section considers the problems faced by struggling pupils as well as the role of computers in literacy. A text that will appeal to teachers, teacher trainers, INSET providers and academics.

Hancock, Joelie (Ed.) *Teaching Literacy Using Information Technology: a Collection of Articles from The Australian Literacy Educators' Association* 132pp. Australian Literacy Educators' Association International Reading Association. ISBN: pbk 087207-198-7. *Available from International Reading Association, 800, Barksdale Road, PO Box 8139, Newark DE 19174 – 8139 USA.*

The limitations and benefits of using technology in educational practice are recognised by this series of re-published, but newly collated papers exploring the potential of literacy development through ICT. Arranged chronologically, the papers exemplify the increasing cultural impact of ICT in education. Each article describes a different aspect of ICT as used in educational settings, providing a rational theoretical perspective on current practice and future implications for teachers. Based upon the premise that teachers need to participate actively in the process of technologising the literacy curriculum, these papers address crucial practicalities and their relationship with fundamental educational issues. The book is relevant to all those involved in the teaching of literacy at all levels.

Harris, Margaret and Hatano, Giyoo (Eds.) *Learning to Read and Write: a Cross-Linguistic Perspective* 252pp. Cambridge and New York: Cambridge University Press. ISBN: hbk 0 521 62184 4.

Although common issues exist, not all the processes involved in learning to read and write are the same in all languages, as they depend in part on the type of script and its associated features. Researchers, post graduate students and teacher trainers wanting to know more about theoretical and empirical aspects of this subject will find much of value in the cross-linguistic perspective taken in the collection of papers described here. Topics covered include phonological awareness, letter knowledge, orthography and syntactic knowledge. The scripts include alphabetic, syllabaries and logographic systems and languages include English, Italian, German, Greek, Hebrew, Japanese and Chinese. Each of the twelve papers concludes with a list of references and an index to all the papers is supplied at the end of the book.

Hawisher, Gail, E and Selfe, Cynthia, L (Eds.) *Global Literacies and the World Wide Web* 299pp. London and New York: Routledge. ISBN: pbk 0 415 18942-X.

Each contribution to this collection emanates from academic research from a different part of the world. The text explores the impact of the web on different communities, highlighting the ways in which web-based texts are used in culturally different ways according to context. Whilst celebrating the dynamic capacity of on-line literacy, it provides challenging reading, showing for example the way cultural identities are reconstituted through the web. This book critically evaluates from a range of perspectives, with major themes being the ambiguity of language, ideology and culture. Researchers involved in the use of ICT, teachers and teacher trainers will be particularly interested in this collection.

Pearson, Jacqueline *Women's Reading in Britain 1750-1835: a Dangerous Recreation* 300pp. Cambridge and New York: Cambridge University Press. ISBN: hbk 0 521 58439 6.

In the late eighteenth and early nineteenth centuries, literacy among women in Britain increased, and they became an important feature of the literary scene. This book explores women's cultural position at the time and investigates the authors who aimed to write for women. A broad overview is counterbalanced by specific studies of women writers including Jane Austen, Ann Radcliffe and Hannah More. Most of the book is concerned with fiction reading. Explored are: male writers' attitudes to female readers; women's reading of different genres and their attendant pleasures and perils; the gendering of library use; reading silently and reading aloud; the impact of class (and to a lesser extent race) on the gendering of reading, and the issue of women's novel reading through the lens of novels which appear to attack it, for example, Jane Austen's Northanger Abbey. Embedded in the text is the paradox that women's reading could be seen as part of their emancipation, while for the labouring classes, women's difficulties in achieving access to literature could be seen as part of their oppression. A wide range of texts which feature women readers are examined, from novels, including the Gothic, conduct books, educational works, letters, journals and memoirs, to texts of politics, economics, history and science. This is a highly scholarly work, with copious notes and an extensive bibliography.

Potter, David S *Literary Texts and the Roman Historian* 218pp. London and New York: Routledge. ISBN: pbk 0 415 0889 8.

This book explores how the literature of Roman times has constructed a version of history which has since been interpreted by historians in a range of ways. Potter explores different types of historical literature, arguing that 'alternative forms of historical narrative' offer alternative paradigms to those intended to be regarded as purely factual. Whilst contributing to the discipline of ancient history, this book also relevantly adds to post-modern literacy arguments, demonstrating how the genre of a text influences interpretation, for example. It explores thoroughly the range of uses of literature and how this has changed over centuries. An enlightening study which, as part of a collection of texts about literacy, presents a refreshing angle. This study might particularly appeal to readers with a historical background who are studying literacy for the first time.

Powell, Rebecca *Literacy as a Moral Imperative: Facing the Challenges of a Pluralistic Society* 151pp. Lanham, Boulder, New York and Oxford: Rowman and Littlefield. ISBN: pbk 0 8476 9459 3.

Powell illustrates how the acquisition of literacy skills is a process of socialisation. She regards all reading and writing events as occurring within a specific linguistic and social context; many children's first encounters with school-based literacy are also their first encounter with ithe hegemonic function of written language' (page 12). She argues that in order to be judged literate, children are obliged to adopt the values of society's dominant groups as inscribed in their literate discourse. Powell's inspirational and convincingly argued work demonstrates the unfairness of the seeming meritocracy of an educational system which teaches a specific way of using language, but which uses a language which suppresses some social groups. She argues for a pedagogy which takes account of pupils' needs to express their own identities through their writing and maintains that they have a right to be taught how to interrogate texts. This book would be of interest to academic researchers and student teachers interested in language and in literacy.

Rassool, Naz *Literacy for Sustainable Development in the Age of Information* 264pp. Clevedon, Philadelphia, Toronto, Sydney, Johannesburg: Multilingual Matters. The Language and Education Library. ISBN: pbk 1 85359 432 6.

This book is divided into three sections, focusing firstly on definitions of literacy and an evaluation of the frameworks which have sought to define it. Secondly it examines the relationship between literacy and social development, exploring the interaction between literacy and language in the pluralist nation-state. It argues strongly that levels of access to different types of literacy are ideologically and politically controlled in different ways in different cultures. Finally it evaluates the adequacy of prevailing definitions of literacy in meeting the complex demands of the current 'information age'. It emphasises that 'Communicative Competence' of individuals needs to be continually updated if those individuals are to interact effectively in a broad context. This book is appropriate for researchers and academics in the fields of literacy, language, sociolinguistics and cultural studies.

Shlain, L (1998) *The Alphabet Versus the Goddess: Male Words and Female Images* 464pp. London: Allen Lane, The Penguin Press, ISBN: hbk 0713 99297 2.

The author proposes that the development of orthography and the movement of communities from oral to literate brought with it physiological changes to the human brain. These changes, the author argues, were a result of increased activity in the left hemisphere of the brain at the expense of activity in the right hemisphere. The book's central thesis is that attributes apparently associated with the left hemisphere – linear, abstract and predominantly masculine – were thus reinforced whilst attributes related to the right – holistic, concrete, visual and feminine – were suppressed. This, it is suggested, led to a fall in status of women and the movement away from matriarchal societies and goddess worship to societies in which patriarchy and misogyny prevailed. Thus the development of literacy is correlated with the changing status of women in society, mythology and religion from the Stone Age until the present day. Schlain concludes by arguing that the advent of visual literacy in the technological age has led to a re-affirmation of the feminine attributes associated with the right hemisphere of the brain. The book draws from a range of subject disciplines including science, anthropology, history and religion and is for readers who are interested in personal and historical accounts of literacy development.

Spitz, Ellen Handler *Inside Picture Books* 320pp. New Haven and London: Yale University Press. ISBN: hbk 0 300 07602 9.

A lecturer in the arts, psychology and culture, the author examines the interactive participation or 'conversational reading' engaged in by adults and children sharing picture books together, and the meanings of this cultural experience in which values are transmitted from one generation to the other. Central themes within the books are investigated, such as bedtime, separation, loss, death, curiosity, disobedience, punishment, identity and self-acceptance. Most of the children's books cited are widely available 'classics' and include, for instance, *The Story of Babar* by Jean de Brunhoff, *Bedtime for Frances* by Russell Hoban, *Where the Wild Things Are* by Maurice Sendak, *Willy the Wimp* by Anthony Browne and *The Story of Little Black Sambo* by Helen Bannerman. A thoughtful account of the meanings transmitted by picture books and their power, this book will be of interest to parents, grandparents, teachers and others working with young children, and to students of children's literature. It includes bibliographical references and an index.

Tyner, K *Literacy in a Digital World: Teaching and Learning in the Age of Information* 291pp. New Jersey: Lawrence Erlbaum Associates, Inc. ISBN: pbk 0 8058 2226 7. *Available in the UK through The Eurospan Group, 3, Henrietta Street, Covent Garden, London, WC2E 8LU, UK.*

This book is written for media education scholars and students and anyone interested in the way new technologies can be integrated into the literacy curriculum. The author takes a historical look at the social and cultural contexts of literacy and argues that new communication technologies have always been initially resisted and then accepted over time. An attempt is made to integrate theories of literacy and mass communication so as to develop a greater understanding of the role of electronic tools in the classroom. The book explores definitions of 'multiliteracies', including media literacy, in the context of new technologies in order to examine the implications for schooled literacy practices. Different approaches to media education, primarily based in US classrooms, are analysed and examples are provided of student-centred media production. The final chapter features two interviews with media educators working in rural and urban North America in which aims and objectives of the media education projects they undertake are discussed.

Wagner, Daniel, A (Ed.) *The Future of Literacy in a Changing World* 417 pp. Cresskill, NJ: Hampton Press. ISBN: hbk 1 57273 082 X. ISBN: pbk 1 57273 083 8. *Available in the UK through the Eurospan Group, 3 Henrietta Street, Covent Garden, London WC2E 8LU.*

This is a revised and updated edition of a publication of the same name published in 1987 by the Pergamon Press, arising from an international conference held by the International Literacy Institute and the National Center on Adult Literacy, at the University of Pennsylvania, set up to advance research and innovation on best practices in literacy in developing countries. Work by leading figures in the field, including Jeanne Chall, John Downing, Dina Feitelson, Dell Hymes, Bambi Schieffelin, Sylvia Scribner, Brian Street, Elizabeth Sulzby and William Teale, are represented. The topics dealt with range from theoretical perspectives on comparative literacy; literacy acquisition in cultural context (including studies looking at literacy learning in Chinese and Japanese, and a study of reading in Brazil); Literacy in multiethnic and multilingual contexts (in Morocco, Israel and the South Pacific); adult literacy in cultural context, and literacy, technology and economic development.

Wagner, Daniel, A, Venezky, Richard, L and Street, Brian, V (Eds.) *Literacy: An International Handbook* 526pp. Colorado and Oxford: Westview Press. ISBN: hbk 0 8133 9058 3.

This volume provides an important reference tool for anyone with an interest in current issues concerning literacy. Written by leading international specialists, the book brings together contributions from major disciplinary fields with an interest in literacy. These cover the age spectrum, examine cultural and geographic diversity, and include historical as well as contemporary perspectives. The introduction signals significant trends in identifying rationales for literacy and areas of debate, whilst at the same time acknowledging the complexity and diversity of differing and wide ranging perspectives. Divided into sections, chapters deal with 'historical and philosophical roots'; 'psychological approaches'; 'sociological and anthropological approaches'; 'language and literacy'; 'curriculum, instruction and assessment'; 'numeracy'; 'policy perspectives'; 'contemporary regional perspectives' and 'literacy and the new technologies'. Each chapter has its own references and there are also comprehensive author and subject indexes.

Walser, Nancy (Ed.) *Reading and Literacy Harvard Education Letter Focus Series* 5 37pp. Cambridge, MA: Harvard College. ISBN: pbk 1 883433 06 1. *Available from: Harvard Education Letter, Gutman Library Suite 349, 6, Appian Way, Cambridge, MA 02138.*

This booklet contains articles on research in literacy previously published in the Harvard Education Letter, which have been revised and updated for publication here. They explore how literacy develops and also examine current strategies for literacy educators. There are sections on reading, writing, spelling and literacy. Topics include first grade reading, school influences on their reading development of low-income children (by Jeanne Chall and Catherine Snow), reading problems, whole language and phonics, language-rich home and school environments, phonemic awareness, writing and high school writing centers, teaching spelling and invented spelling, culture and literacy, and multimedia tools as a scaffold for the disabled. With its helpful references, this booklet will be of interest to researchers in the literacy field.

Werth, Paul *Text Worlds: Representing Conceptual Space in Discourse* 390pp. London and New York: Longman: An imprint of Pearson Education. ISBN: pbk 0 582 22914 6.

The way texts work to create 'new worlds' is explored in this book. Werth investigates the complex ways in which readers interact with text in order to make sense of both the text and the world beyond it. The study demonstrates in painstaking detail how texts work, showing the relationships within the lexicon of the texts themselves and the manner in which these relationships create new meanings for readers who enter that textual world or 'conceptual domain'. This book will be of interest to all those interested in literary theory, literary criticism and linguistics. It also crosses disciplines into psychology and the philosophy of language and as such is likely to have a broad appeal, despite its very technical approach to reading and language.

Wheale, Nigel *Writing and Society: Literacy, Print and Politics in Britain 1590-1660*, 188pp. London and New York: Routledge. ISBN: pbk 0 415 08498 9.

This book catalogues changes in the use of written language in the 'early modern period' of British history. It details the growth of popular literacy and explores the links between new readerships and the authors and texts which addressed them. The main themes reviewed are: the development of literacy by status, gender and region in Britain; the structures of patronage and censorship; the role of the publishing industry; the relationship between elite literacy and popular cultures; the growth of female literacy and publication; and the impact of English state policies on Celtic literary cultures. There are many facsimile pages from influential books of the period and a year-by-year chronology of political events in relation to literacy and cultural production.

Literacy in the Early and Primary Years

Anning, Angela, and Edwards, Anne *Promoting Children's Learning from Birth to Five: Developing the New Early Years Professional* 184pp. Buckingham and Philadelphia: Open University Press. ISBN: hbk 0 335 20217 9. ISBN: pbk 0 335 20216 0.

Although this is not principally a book about literacy, it is included here because it reports a research project which aimed to develop and articulate a model for effective education in literacy and mathematics for very young children, and it contains two key chapters on 'language and literacy learning' and 'How adults support children's literacy learning'. At a time of great change in pre-school provision, this book draws on research undertaken by practitioners in conjunction with university-based researchers, in a range of early years settings, to offer a helpful framework for providing suitable literacy curriculum experiences for infants. This book will be useful for those working in early years and family services developing literacy curricula for young children.

Browne, Naima *Young Children's Literacy Development and the Role of Televisual Texts* 208 pp. London and New York: Falmer Press. ISBN: hbk 0 7507 0855 7. ISBN: pbk 0 7507 0856 5.

This study presents a clear view of the ways young children's early literacy development can be supported by their experiences of videos, particularly those that are narrative based. Questionnaires, semi-structured interviews and observation were employed to explore issues of whether watching television discourages reading; why some children prefer to watch television than read books; the influence of television and videos on children's writing development, and the impact of gender and children's, parents' and teachers' views on the positive and negative aspects of television and videos. The children in the study, several of whom were emergent bilinguals, were aged between four and seven and attended six schools. The information about children's use of television and videos is considered from a school perspective on how teachers use television and videos at school and their views of children's home viewing experiences. Questionnaires used and examples of transcripts of taped interviews are provided. A thought-provoking book in an important field, this publication will be helpful for those teaching literacy to young children.

Campbell, Robin *Literacy from Home to School: Reading with Alice* 168 pp. Stoke on Trent: Trentham. ISBN: pbk 1 85856 166 3. *In North America available from Stylus Publishing.*

This is a case study chronicling the first five years of the literacy development of the author's grand-daughter. Through the engaging narrative which depicts the particular, the seemingly mundane and the epiphanous moments of Alice's development, Campbell demonstrates the usefulness of case study as a research method. Using a combination of transcripted conversation and examples of early attempts at writing and drawing, the author carefully identifies the significance of apparently trivial events which add up to the rich experiences of this fortunate infant. Parents, early years teachers and student teachers will find the text enlightening, as will researchers interested in investigating the value of case study methods.

Department for Education and Employment *The National Literacy Strategy Revision Guidance for Year 6 pupils: Suggested Lesson Plans* 10pp. London: DfEE Product Code: RGY6SLP. *Available free from Department for Education and Employment, Sanctuary Buildings, Great Smith Street, London SW1 3BT.*

Department for Education and Employment *The National Literacy Strategy Revision Guidance for Year 6 pupils: Activity Resource Sheets* 64pp. London: DfEE. ISBN: pbk 0 19 312194 8.

Department for Education and Employment *The National Literacy Strategy: Phonics Progression in Phonics: Materials for Whole Class Teaching* 123 pp. London: DfEE. ISBN: pbk 0 19 312237 5.

Department for Education and Employment *The National Literacy Strategy: Spelling Bank: Lists of Words and Activities for the KS2 Spelling Objectives* 87pp. London: DfEE. ISBN: pbk 0 19 312240 5.

Department for Education and Employment *The National Literacy Strategy Training Modules 4 Phonics YR and Y1 Approximately 50 (un-numbered)* pp. London: DfEE. ISBN: pbk 0 19 312238 3.

Department for Education and Employment *The National Literacy Strategy Training Modules 5 Spelling Key Stage 2 Approximately 50 (un-numbered)* pp. London: DfEE. ISBN: pbk 0 19 312241 3.

All available from Department for Education and Employment, Sanctuary Buildings, Great Smith Street, London SW1 3BT.

In addition to providing lesson plans and resources, these booklets set out brief rationales for the structured approach to the teaching of literacy. Ways of involving children in collecting words that illustrate spelling rules (Year 6) and ways of helping children to learn word patterns (Year 3) for example, are demonstrated. Overhead transparency templates are provided, to illustrate vowel sounds, phonemes and consonant blends for example, as well as whole words and lists of words or short sentences. The emphasis is upon structured and careful presentations, the use of technical language to encourage self-conscious learning, and there is an assumption of logical progress. The books are aimed at classroom teachers involved in teaching the literacy hour in the context of the National Literacy Strategy.

Drever, Mina, Moule, Susan and Peterson, Keith *Teaching English in Primary Classrooms* 190pp. Stoke on Trent: Trentham Books. ISBN: pbk 1 85856 177 9. In North America available from Stylus Publishing.

This book outlines a range of approaches to exploring language and the ways it works with primary school children. The strategies used by teachers in this book were originally designed specifically for use with bilingual pupils. However, the teachers who used them found that the activities worked successfully with monolingual pupils and so they are presented here for use with all pupils in primary schools, whatever their linguistic repertoire. The book expounds the theoretical principles underpinning the pedagogical approaches taken by the authors and includes a rationale for the collaborative approach to learning that features in many of the lessons. The introductory chapters also emphasise the need for explicitly teaching grammar and stress the importance of locating grammar within a meaningful context for children. The authors then move on to detail a series of lessons on a variety of topics related to knowledge about language at text, sentence and word level. Examples of children's work are featured throughout the book.

Fisher, Ros and Arnold, Helen (Eds.) *Understanding the Literacy Hour*
97pp. Royston: United Kingdom Reading Association (UKRA). ISBN:
pbk 1 897638 23 X. *Available from: Unit 6, 1st Floor, The Maltings,
Green Drift, Royston, Herts. SG8 5DB, UK.*

The series of papers collected here emanates from a conference about the
National Literacy Strategy before its official implementation in 1998. The papers
have since been revised to reflect thoughts a few months after implementation.
The first section concentrates on the rationale, roots and aims of the Literacy
Hour as well as including a summary of its characteristics and form. The second
section reflects on actual classroom practice and provides practical strategies
for teaching, including ways of incorporating poetry and ICT into the structure.
This collection ends with a piece each by Fisher and Arnold, who offer
cautionary advice about the wholesale importation of a strategy to suit all pupils'
needs, warning that it could culminate in an ossified curriculum. This book provides an overview of the Literacy Hour provided by those who have helped
develop or pilot it.

Garton, Alison, and Pratt, Chris *Learning to be Literate: the Development of Spoken and Written Language* (2nd edition) 300pp. Oxford and
Malden, Massachusetts: Blackwell Publishers. ISBN: pbk 0 631 19317 0.

This is the second edition of a book first published in 1989. The authors define
literacy as 'the mastery of spoken language and reading and writing'. They state
their intention to explore the relationships between oral and written language
development up to around age eight. Of the ten chapters, six are principally concerned with describing research into the processes and achievements of oral
language development. There are then two chapters summarising research into
learning to write and into learning to read. The final, short chapter reflects on
the nature and consequences of literacy development. Much of the book actually
treats oral and written language development independently but relationships
between the two are discussed explicitly in the opening and concluding chapters
and at some other points. Like the first edition, the book provides a basic introduction to both aspects of language development within a single volume.

Geekie, Peter, Cambourne, Brian and Fitzsimmons, Phil *Understanding Literacy Development* 233pp. Stoke on Trent: Trentham. ISBN: pbk 1 85856 08661. *In North America available from Stylus Publishing.*

This book draws on videotaped longitudinal research from Australian primary school literacy sessions and explores in detail the written and spoken language of pupils engaged in learning to read and write. The authors emphasise the need for teachers to understand pupils' strategies for learning and to invest in these as the main focus of their teaching. Through the use of transcribed pupil discussions and written work, the strategies children develop themselves to aid their own learning are highlighted. The writers urge teachers to invest in these strategies and nurture pupils' emergent skills, allowing them the time to question and investigate and to help one another in print-rich environments.

Goodwin, Prue (Ed.) *The Literate Classroom* **144pp. London: David Fulton Publishers.** ISBN: pbk 1 85346 566 6. *Available in North America from Taylor and Francis.*

The diverse collection of research-based chapters explores the reading and writing of pupils right across the primary sector. The contributors offer practical guidance and strategies for use in the classroom whilst highlighting their relationship to current educational debates in the UK. Each chapter focuses on a different initiative or aspect of literacy teaching whilst emphasising literacy as the fundamental issue in the primary classroom. The National Literacy Strategy is celebrated by some of these writers, who are directly involved in its implementation and who indicate its roots in previous research and good practice; other authors indicate its omissions and oversights. Teachers, researchers and those involved in training would find this text a rich resource of well-justified and illustrated ideas.

Hinson, Mike (Ed.) *Surviving the Literacy Hour* 59pp. Tamworth, Staffs.: NASEN. ISBN: pbk 1 901485 03 X. *Available from NASEN House, 4/5 Amber Business Village, Amber Close, Amington, Tamworth, Staffs., B77 4RP, UK.*

The contributors to this edited volume share their thoughts and experiences about the implementation of the National Literacy Strategy in UK primary schools. Offering reflections upon and ideas for strategies to cope with the management of pupils and their learning, the writers cautiously outline the difficulties they have faced in coping with new ways of working in the UK and share professional expertise for the benefit of other practitioners. It offers a useful insight for researchers in the field as to how the Literacy Hour is being received by teachers in schools, as well as ideas for teachers wishing to find practical support from fellow practitioners.

Her Majesty's Stationery Office (HMSO) *The National Literacy Strategy: An Interim Evaluation* 10pp. London: HMSO. Available free from OFSTED Publication Centre, PO Box 6927, London E3 3NZ.

This report is based upon evidence gathered from 138 UK primary schools in the spring term of 1999 and is interim to a full report planned for the autumn term. It does not reflect upon the strategy itself, but upon the teaching, management and reception of it. Its recommendations therefore focus on improvements concerning the better training of teachers and headteachers in the teaching of particular aspects of the Literacy Hour. The criteria for assessment used in the evaluation are not described and quantitative and brief judgements are made, such as through the use of statistics about 'good' or 'satisfactory' teaching.

Lloyd, Peta, Mitchell, Helena and Monk, Jenny (Eds.) *The Literacy Hour and Language Knowledge* 102pp. London: David Fulton Publishers. ISBN: pbk 1 85346 578 X. *Available in North America from Taylor and Francis.*

This book supports the new Literacy Hour as recently introduced into the English National Curriculum and provides detailed strategies for ways of harnessing the creative potential of poetry and stories within the parameters of the Literacy Hour. In reminding readers of the richness of these genres and of the need to develop pupils' critical awareness, the book details techniques for working with whole classes on particular aspects of specified texts. Taking the categories of word, sentence and whole text level (as stipulated in the National Literacy Strategy) the book carefully identifies ways in which all these can be encompassed without losing sight of the overall creative potential of the texts under scrutiny. Useful for teachers and co-ordinators working with the Literacy Hour, as well as all those who are interested in taking a more systematic approach to primary teaching of Literacy.

Marsh, Jackie and Hallet, Elaine (Eds.) *Desirable Literacies: Approaches to Language and Literacy in the Early Years* 233pp. London, Thousand Oaks: Paul Chapman, a SAGE Publications Company. ISBN: hbk 1 85396 446 8. pbk 1 85396 447 6.

The introduction to this comprehensive research-based collection of writings about the teaching of 3-8 year olds reminds readers that 'There is no single road to becoming literate' (Goodman 1997: 56). As testimony to this the writers critically evaluate different avenues of literacy teaching based on their own experiences and observations. Some chapters provide an overview of much debated topics within the sphere of literacy and language work, such as the role of talk, the development of writing and Drama. Others open up newer areas, such as the role of ICT or popular culture (most notably Marsh's work on 'Teletubbies'). The text is aimed at teachers of early literacy as well as student teachers and those who work with them.

References: Goodman, Y. (1997) 'Multiple Roads to Literacy' in D, Taylor (Ed.) *Many Families, Many Literacies*. New Hampshire: Heinemann.

Merchant, Guy and Thomas, Huw (Eds.) *Picture Books for the Literacy Hour: Activities for Primary Teachers* 133pp. David Fulton Publishers: London. ISBN: pbk 1 85346 627 1. *Available in North America from Taylor and Francis.*

This book celebrates the value of picture books as a means for the development of literacy. It provides readers with a rationale for the selection of high quality texts and examines how their potential can be exploited in the literacy classroom. The multi-layered levels of meaning in specific books are outlined as a way of illustrating the depth of picture books and the way in which complex ideas are made accessible to young readers. The writers offer a range of up-to-date ideas of working with picture books with primary age children and in particular suggest strategies of incorporating such work into the Literacy Hour as outlined by the National Literacy Strategy in the UK.

Miller, Linda *Moving Towards Literacy with Environmental Print* Minibook 11, 32pp. Royston, Herts., UKRA United Kingdom Reading Association. ISBN: pbk 1 897638 17 5 *Available from: Unit 6, 1st Floor, The Maltings, Green Drift, Royston, Herts. SG8 5DB, UK*

A helpful minibook for teachers, students teachers and parents which provides accessible information about ways of responding to environmental print in an early years context. This includes a review of relevant research, the role of the adult in relation to environmental print, projects involving parents, and a discussion of environmental print diaries. The implications for early years settings of research on environmental print are discussed, incorporating a look at the literacy hour and suggestions for conducting a print audit, and there is a short section on assessment. The material may be photocopied, with acknowledgement. There are four pages of references for further study.

Moorcroft, Christine *Responding to Stories: Learning Activities for Early Years* 64 pp. London: A and C Black. ISBN 1 7136 4855 4. *Available from 35, Bedford Row, London, WC1R 4JH UK.*

This text comprises a series of ideas for literacy activities which can be used to encourage young children's pre-school literacy development. Coinciding with guidelines offered by the Qualifications and Curriculum Authority on Desirable Outcomes for children's pre-school development, each activity is exemplified, learning outcomes are identified and strategies for assessment suggested. Differentiation and extension activities are also offered for some of the activities and it is through these suggestions that some limited academic commentary about literacy is offered.

Office for Standards in Education (OFSTED) *Primary Follow-up Survey of the Training of Trainee Teachers to Teach Number and Reading 1996-1998* 59 pp London: OFSTED HMI ref no: HMI 193. *In the UK available free from OFSTED Publication Centre, PO Box 6927, London E3 34NZ UK.*

All seventy-two Initial Teacher Training Providers for primary school teachers in the UK were included in this survey of training for the teaching of Number and Reading. A four point scale (very good, good, adequate, poor) was used to evaluate the provision and training offered by courses in order to meet the statutory Standards for Initial Teacher Training. The results of the survey are organised according to the sections described by the Standards (OFSTED and TTA 1996). Methodology is not described and terms such as 'a few', 'most' or 'a minority' are not defined but regularly used. Literacy and number teaching is discussed simultaneously. Those who are interested in the inspection process in the UK or involved in teacher training would find this report of interest.

Pahl, Kate *Transformations: Meaning Making in Nursery Education* 110pp. Stoke on Trent: Trentham Books. ISBN: pbk 1 85856 098 5. *In North America available form Stylus Publishing.*

A very clearly presented and carefully thought out text on young children making meanings in a multi-modal way, this book will be of interest to educators of children under five and their parents. The book is based on an observational study of children in a small multi-cultural inner-city nursery and examines the design of the children's models in order to come to an understanding of the decisions children reach about form and structure, and more generally, representation. Here literacy is seen as part of a whole landscape of communication, including play, talk, writing, drawing, collage and modelling. Photographs and other reproductions of the children's work support the text. Since Kate Pahl is a parent of one of the children she was also to see what happened to certain work when it was taken home. Building on theoretical models of children's learning and previous research, the book is an excellent resource for students of literacy and contains a helpful bibliography. Policy and practice issues are also addressed, including boys' literacy development and links between home and school.

Richards, Janet C and Gipe, Joan P *Elementary Literacy Lessons: Cases and Commentaries from the Field* 231pp. London: Lawrence Erlbaum Associates. ISBN: pbk 0 8058 2988 1.

This book comprises a collection of brief case studies taken from the experiences of beginner teachers struggling with the teaching of literacy. It begins with a discussion of what a case study is and to what use such studies can be put. It is argued that student teachers can learn a great deal from anecdotes of teaching experiences but that a case study should demonstrate specific points. Accordingly, the book serves two main purposes: firstly, it provides a series of case studies with commentaries from experienced teachers from which student teachers can learn about literacy teaching, secondly, it demonstrates the potential of case study work as a research and a pedagogical tool. Each study is followed by a series of questions to prompt discussion and by a number of commentaries. A useful book for student teachers, newly qualified teachers and their mentors or trainers, it is in addition it is a useful model for researchers interested in embarking on case study work.

Richards, Janet C and Gipe, Joan P *Facilitator's Manual to Accompany Elementary Literacy Lessons: Cases and Commentaries* **from the Field** 70pp. London: Lawrence Erlbaum Associates. ISBN: pbk 0 8058 3457 5.

This manual accompanies *Elementary Literacy Lessons: Cases and Commentaries from the Field*. It is addressed to mentors or trainers and identifies the case study as a rich pedagogical resource. It provides sample responses to questions which are asked about the case studies provided in Elementary Literacy Lessons as well as an introductory section which advises generally about the use of case study work.

Sedgwick, Fred *Thinking about Literacy: Young Children and their Language* 174pp. London and New York: Routledge. ISBN: pbk 0 415 16865 1.

This book aims to widen the debate about children's literacy beyond the literacy hour. Part I addresses aspects of talking, from early talk, illustrated by a case study of a three-year-old boy, to talk in the infants school, and a section on children asking questions about moral issues. An intervening section looks at children making their own books. Part 2 is about writing, influenced by the work of Frank Smith. There are chapters on the writing corner, letter writing (between the author and six-year-old children), writing lists and a chapter on secretarial issues. The final Part explores reading, with a chapter on different approaches from a political standpoint, and one recording the recollections of a number of people about how they learnt to read. A postscript looks at the National Curriculum for England and Wales and an OFSTED report. The book is full of children's own words, writing and drawing, and shows how they are very actively engaged in their literacy learning.

Wade, Barrie and Moore, Maggie (1998) *Bookstart: the First Five Years – a Description and Evaluation of an Exploratory British Project to Encourage Sharing Books with Babies* 56pp. London: Book Trust. ISBN: pbk 0 853353 470 5. *Available from: Young Book Trust, Book House, 45, East Hill, London, SW18 2QZ.*

This booklet gives details about the Bookstart Project, a scheme which encourages parents to share books with babies from a young age, first initiated in 1992 in Birmingham, and now available more widely in Britain. The history of the project is described, and issues about who the scheme is for, timing, materials, organisation, and funding are all addressed. Feedback and evaluations are offered from projects already underway and details are given of planned projects, together with contact details. References and details of a survey form for collecting information about projects are provided. This booklet will be useful to anyone intending to work on a Bookstart project or who is interested in the idea of books for babies.

Waters, Mick and Martin, Tony *Co-ordinating English at Key Stage Two* 243pp. London and Philadelphia: Falmer Press, Taylor and Francis Group. ISBN: pbk 0 7507 0686 4.

This is a handbook with a strong emphasis on practical advice to teachers working in schools. Securely cognisant of current curriculum requirements and inspection processes, the text advises literacy co-ordinators and subject leaders on a range of strategies for developing children's literacy. The authors illustrate their advice with up-to-date examples and illustrations taken from a range of schools. The text is highly amenable to selective reading, but also provides a thorough and well-grounded comprehensive 'training ground', particularly for teachers who have taken on new responsibilities. Preparation for inspection, assessment, target setting and Schemes of Work are all included, as are policy issues and staff management. Examples of pupils' work provide a fine focus for literacy analysis and epitomise the authors' evident determination to maintain pupils' needs as central to all work in schools.

Whitehead, Marian *Supporting Language and Literacy Development in the Early Years* 154pp. Buckingham and Philadelphia: Open University Press. ISBN: hbk 0 335 19932 1. ISBN: pbk 0 335 19931 3.

Those concerned with the care and education of children from birth to six years will find this book of interest. Marian Whitehead not only presents a developmental view of language but also discuses the emergence of literacy and the role of both literature and environmental print in these years. Permeating the book is the notion of language and education as shared community endeavours, so notes are provided at the end of relevant chapters which give practical suggestions for supporting children's development. Further, she offers a case study of two distinctive approaches to early literacy, one evolved from the British nursery school, the other from Steiner Waldorf traditions. These lead her to consider the current national frameworks for literacy highly critically and to analyse ways in which the understanding of providers may be narrowed and children's experience restricted by them.

Literacy in the Secondary Years

Butler, Michael and Keith, George *Language, Power and Identity* (Living Language Series) 121pp. London: Hodder and Stoughton. ISBN: pbk 0 340 73085 4. *Available from Hodder and Stoughton Educational, 338 Euston Road, London, NW1 3BH.*

Intended for a readership of A' level and GNVQ students, this text would nevertheless be useful to a broader audience of teachers, students and those interested in the ways in which power and identity are encoded into language. Consumerism in texts is a central theme and this is explored through the lenses of gender, citizenship and culture. Drawing on a linguistics paradigm, the text provides technical vocabulary and strategies to explore the ideological assumptions in a wide range of texts. It explains to and asks questions of readers. Also provided are references to texts for further study.

Davison, Jon and Moss, John (Eds.) *Issues in English Teaching* 289pp. London and New York: Routledge. ISBN: hbk 0 415 20664 2. ISBN: pbk 0 415 20665 0.

Each of the chapters in this highly contemporary collection focuses upon a key issue in English and contextualises it within current debate and practices. Eleven of its fifteen chapter titles end with a question mark, indicating the controversial nature of the topics and the enquiring stance of the authors. The status of reading, writing and talk are each reviewed, as are Drama, the place of critical theory and the canon. Crucial arguments about linguistic appropriacy, the place of Standard English and English as a global language are all embraced in a text which will be valuable to student teachers of English in both the primary and secondary sectors. The dimensions of class and gender are also addressed in this comprehensive text.

Department for Education and Employment *The National Literacy Strategy Guidance for Providers of Summer Literacy Schools and Key Stage 3 Intervention Programmes for Literacy 1999-2000* 39pp. London: DfEE Product Code: RGY6SLP. *Available free from Department for Education and Employment, Sanctuary Buildings, Great Smith Street, London SW1 3BT.*

Improving children's literacy skills is at the heart of the British Government's determination to raise standards of pupil achievement. The National Literacy Strategy is a relatively new innovation and therefore many pupils who will be transferring from Primary Schools in the year 2000 will not have been taught through the literacy hour during all their primary years. The government has therefore funded 'Literacy Schools' for the third year running, in order to 'deliver' intervention programmes and 'fill the gaps in the literacy skills of pupils who have failed to reach level 4' (page 3). This is a self-contained fifty-hour programme to develop pupils' literacy skills in readiness for entry to secondary school education. The responsibility of secondary schools with regard to pupils' literacy development and monitoring is clearly outlined, including the need to liase with Primary Schools and to incorporate aspects of the literacy hour in their teaching during the summer school programmes. (Information on the evaluation of this initiative can be found in Sainsbury, Marian; Caspall, Louise; McDonald, Angus; Ravenscroft, Lesley and Schagen, Ian *Evaluation of the 1998 Summer Schools Programme: Full Report* in the section on Assessment.)

Department for Education and Employment *The National Literacy Strategy: Key Stage Three Literacy Conferences LEA file* 106pp. London: DfEE. ISBN: 019 312281 2.

Department for Education and Employment *The National Literacy Strategy: Key Stage Three Literacy Conferences School File* 42pp. London: DfEE. ISBN: 019 312228 6.

All available from Department for Education and Employment, Sanctuary Buildings, Great Smith Street, London SW1 3BT.

These files provide training notes and overhead transparency templates for use in developing policies in secondary schools for the development of pupils' literacy across the curriculum. Based upon the National Literacy Strategy used in primary schools, the programmes advocate a structured approach but one which is more flexible than that used in primary schools. The research of Wray and Lewis (1997) is invoked as are the use of Directed Activities Related to Texts (Lunzer and Gardner 1979) and Writing Frames (Lewis and Wray, 1988). The need is highlighted to raise teachers' awareness about the relationship between language and learning as well as consideration of the features of writing used typically across subject areas. These files are targeted at Local Education Authority trainers and secondary school literacy co-ordinators in the UK; they will also be of interest to literacy policy researchers and teacher trainers.

References: Lewis, Maureen and Wray, David (1988) *Writing Across The Curriculum: Frames to Support Learning* University of Reading: Reading Language and Information Centre.

Lunzer, E. and Gardner, K. (1979) *The Effective Use of Reading* London: Heinemann.

Wray, David and Lewis, Maureen (1997) *Extending Literacy: Children Reading and Writing Non-fiction* London: Routledge.

Goodwyn, Andrew (Ed.) *Literacy and Media Texts in Secondary English* 152 pp. London and New York: Cassell Education. ISBN: pbk 0 304 70359 1.

The chapters in this collection each considers creative ways of teaching English by accommodating the strictures of a legislated curriculum whilst making the process of reading contemporary and purposeful. Goodwyn's introduction argues that the 'controlling forces'of education are locked into a nostalgic, monolithic view of literacy, whereas students require support in making sense of an increasingly culturally and linguistically diverse multimedia world. The book challenges institutional views of what it means to be 'well read', urging teachers to reject a reductive and elite definition of literacy. The research-based chapters demonstrate a flexible way of teaching the English curriculum, showing ways of approaching texts by fostering a critical literacy approach with a broad range of texts. A highly relevant contribution to the debate about literacy in secondary curricula, which also offers a way forward for teachers frustrated by ever- increasing governmental intervention and narrowing of the English curriculum.

Jago, Michael *Language and Style* (Living Language Series) 119pp. London: Hodder and Stoughton. ISBN: pbk 0 340 73082 X. *Available from Hodder and Stoughton Educational, 338 Euston Road, London, NW1 3BH.*

This book demonstrates ways of analysing different types of non-fiction text through exemplification, commentaries and exercises. Intended for A' level and GNVQ students, the book would nevertheless be useful to the many trainees and teachers who are increasingly required to develop critical skills of textual analysis. Technical terms are explained and exemplified so that readers quickly equip themselves with a range of investigative skills for the deconstruction of texts. References provided at the end of each chapter also include short indicative commentaries so that readers can research further. This introductory text is rich with examples from a broad range of literature and would provide a useful reference text as well as a teaching resource.

Lewis, Maureen and Wray, David (Eds.) *Literacy in the Secondary School* 182pp. London: David Fulton Publishers. ISBN: pbk1 85346 655 7. Available in North America from Taylor and Francis.

This collection begins with a series of chapters authored by the editors themselves, offering a comprehensive history to the currently strong government focus on literacy in the UK. They highlight the pros and cons of a new parliament that has education as its highest agenda item. The plethora of well-intended literacy initiatives are evaluated and it is made clear that secondary schools have much ground to cover in comparison to their primary school counterparts when the Literacy Strategy 'moves up'. Descriptions of Wray and Lewis's own EXCEL project (see Wray and Lewis, 1997) lead into a series of chapters by teachers from a range of subject disciplines offering accounts of their own classroom practice of teaching literacy through the medium of a variety of subject areas. The text will be suitable for teachers involved in initial and in-service training, their tutors and all those involved in literacy development at Local Education Authority or school level.

Reference: Wray, D. and Lewis, M. (1997) *Extending Literacy: Children Reading and Writing Non-fiction* London and New York: Routledge.

Strong, Julia *Literacy at 11-14: A Practical Guide to Raising Achievement through Whole School Literacy Development* 144pp. London: Collins Educational. ISBN: pbk 000 323 080 5.

The author of this guide for literacy co-ordinators, teachers, in-service educators, literacy governors and senior management of secondary schools, is the Deputy Director of the National Literacy Trust of the UK. Drawing on her research and experience as both an INSET trainer and teacher of English, she presents a whole range of strategies and ideas for developing a literacy policy to reach across the whole curriculum in secondary schools. She provides a rationale for the work she suggests and indicates a number of routes for schools to take, depending upon the current situation in those schools. She begins with the basics, describing the purpose of such a policy and how departments can audit their current *modus operandi* before mobilising into action. The book is practical in nature and includes a large number of OHT templates for use in training and in teaching. All of these are well described with clear indications of the advantages and disadvantages of the various activities and strategies. This is a timely and useful publication which will also have a place in the hands of teacher trainers.

Literacy for Young Adults and Adults

Basic Skills Agency (BSA) *Effective Basic Skills Provision for Adults* 36pp. London: Basic Skills Agency. ISBN 1 85990 096 8. *Available free from: The Basic Skills Agency, Commonwealth House, 1-19, New Oxford Street, London, WC1A 1NU.*

This report has been written for basic skills programme providers. It discusses the quality of provision, teaching methods and materials, assessment, and staffing for basic skills. Previous Adult Literacy and Basic Skills Unit (ALBSU) and BSA surveys are used to support the policies and recommendations put forward. It will be useful for providers seeking to meet the BSA Basic Skills Quality Mark for Post-16 programmes in the UK, as it relates to a number of Quality Mark elements and gives specific advice in relation to them.

Basic Skills Agency *1997-8 Annual Report* 20pp. London: Basic Skills Agency. ISBN 1 85990 087 9. *Available free from: The Basic Skills Agency, Commonwealth House, 1-19, New Oxford Street, London, WC1A 1NU.*

A short publication, this gives details of the current working of the Basic Skills Agency in England and Wales, outlining the achievements made within the year, the ways they set about achieving their aims, the development of learning opportunities, ways of helping to improve effectiveness, the dissemination of practice, ways of operating and how the budget has been spent. There is a list of the Board of Management and staff.

Mawer, Giselle *Workplace Education: Learning at Work* 304pp. London and New York: Longman. ISBN hbk 0 582 25764 6. ISBN: pbk 0 582 25765 4.

This is a study of the practical and conceptual challenges involved in education and training in the workplace. Through a series of case studies, it explores different approaches to adult education at work. The author interweaves theoretical and practical considerations and illustrates the issues carefully. The text shows how it is possible to develop individual workers' skills and also to integrate the development of language, literacy and cross-cultural issues in the process of that learning. As part of Longman's Language and Literacy series, there is a strong focus on linguistic communicative issues, yet these are discussed in an accessible manner. This text would be of relevance and use to those working in the fields of adult education, vocational training, and linguistics, as well as to specialists in literacy.

Moser, Claus *Improving Literacy and Numeracy: A Fresh Start. The Report of the Working Group chaired by Sir Claus Moser* 108pp. London: Department for Education and Employment. ISBN: 1 84185 005 5. *Available from: DfEE Publications. PO Box 5050, Sudbury, Suffolk, CO10 6ZQ. Tel 0845 60 222 60.*

This report has been produced by the Working Group on Post-School Basic Skills. The Working Group's terms of reference focus on advising on ways in which the Government's plans for basic skills provision can be implemented so that Government targets can be met. Throughout the report, the major emphasis is on economic aspects of basic skills. Part 1 of the report describes the perceived problem and the Working Group's strategy for dealing with it. Part 2 discusses the scale of need; the impact of poor basic skills and the current situation. Part 3, the major part of the report, considers ways of increasing participation; entitlement to quality learning opportunities; effective programmes; new qualifications for basic skills; local partnerships; national co-ordination; funding, and research and development. The report concludes with recommendations and a list of 'Official' and Basic Skills Agency references.

Vogel, Susan A. and Reder, Stephen (Eds.) (1998) *Learning Disabilities, Literacy, and Adult Education* 377pp. Baltimore, USA and London, UK: Paul H. Brookes Publishing Co. ISBN: pbk 1 55766 347 5.

This collection of papers combining theoretical and practical approaches will be of interest to educators, teacher trainers, literacy providers, policy makers and educational psychologists. The central thrust of the book is the relation of learning disability to literacy acquisition. Four general papers introduce background issues. Section 2, on screening and assessment, gives details of several screening and diagnostic procedures. Instructional strategies are described in Section 3 and employment issues in Section 4. Future directions are summarised in Section 5. References are provided at the end of each paper and an index completes the book. Useful appendices include information resources and clearing houses for North America and a product resources list of technology, including computer software.

BOOKS ON PARTICULAR STRANDS OF LITERACY

Focus on Reading

Barrs, Myra and Pidgeon, Sue (Eds.) *Boys and Reading 49pp. London: Centre for Language in Primary Education*. ISBN: pbk 1 8722 67 14 9. *Available from CLPE, Webber Street, London SE1 8QW. Tel: 0171 401 3382/3.*

A well-produced and attractively presented publication which explores current issues and provides practical suggestions on the timely topic of helping boys to engage more fully with the reading process. The authors of the articles here work or have contact with primary and secondary schools in and around the London area, but the issues they raise have resonance within a wider context. This booklet will be particularly useful for teachers and teachers in training who are concerned about extending the work of the boys they teach. Photographs and illustrations enliven the publication, and key references are provided.

Bielby, Nicholas *Teaching Reading at Key Stage* 2 209pp. Cheltenham: Stanley Thornes. ISBN: pbk 0 7487 4040 6. Available from Stanley Thornes Publishers Ltd., Ellenborough House, Wellington Street, Cheltenham, Gloucester, GL5 1YW.

This is a thorough and well presented outline of teaching reading for practising teachers and those in training. The book draws on current research findings on the development of children's literacy skills. The objectives which each chapter aims to address are clearly stated, summaries at the end of each chapter are provided and implications for practice discussed. Key words are flagged in the margins, and the book also contains a helpful glossary of terms. The topics dealt with are: children and the reading process; children and their reading; children construing meaning; reading stories; reading poetry; information and study skills, and assessment and intervention. Academic references, and also references to literary works, including children's literature, are supplied. Like the other books in the series, this publication addresses the requirements of the National Literacy Strategy and the ITT National Curriculum. It would be a helpful text to use in teacher training.

Burns, Susan, M, Griffin, Peg and Snow, Catherine E (Eds.) *Starting Out Right; a Guide to Promoting Children's Reading Success* 182pp. Washington, DC: National Academy Press. ISBN: pbk 0 309 06410 4. *Available in the UK from National Academy Press including Henry Joseph Press, Plymouth Distributors Ltd. Estover, Plymouth PL6 7PZ or 12 Hids Copse Road, Cumnor Hill, Oxford, OX2 9JJ, UK.*

This is an attractively produced 'how to' book aimed at parents, teachers and others who work with and care for young children. It contains over 50 activities to do with children to excite them about different aspects and skills involved in reading. There is a list of American-published children's books, a guide to computer and CD ROM software and a list of internet resources, recommended by the National Research Council in the USA. The book begins with a discussion of the circumstances which can promote reading in young children and then examines reading development through various phases: birth to four and then the early years of school. Practical activities and checklists of skills are provided throughout the book, for each particular phase of reading development. There is some theoretical underpinning, though this is not extensive and the book is largely practical in nature. There is also a chapter on 'Preventing Reading Difficulties', a section discussing the importance of community and a glossary of technical terms.

Edwards, Sylvia *Reading for All* 90pp. London: David Fulton. ISBN: pbk 1 85346 601 8. Available in North America from Taylor and Francis.

This text embraces the National Literacy Strategy (currently in its second year in UK schools) and predominately targets an audience of primary school teachers in the UK. In an endorsement of recent government interventional strategies in UK schools, the book shows how general standards of literacy can be raised via careful implementation of the government literacy framework. In addition to offering guidance on policy writing and interpretation of government orders, it also offers well researched strategies for use in the classroom. There is a specific accent on teaching pupils with Special Educational Needs, with ideas for differentiation and the creation of resources.

Guthrie, John, T and Alvermann, Donna, E (Ed.) *Engaged Reading: Processes, Practices and Policy Implications* 178pp. New York and London: Teachers College Press. ISBN: pbk 0 8077 3816 6. *Available in the UK through the Eurospan Group, 3 Henrietta Street, Covent Garden, London WC2E 8LU.*

The chapters in this book, all focused on different aspects of engagement in reading, are based on studies of reading conducted at the National Reading Research Center. They explore historical and political contexts; the processes of motivated readers; reading at different stages in school and the teaching implications that arise; opportunities for reading at home and in the community; issues of studying engaged reading and the methodologies employed, and what reading engagement means for school reform. This is a scholarly book, offering a rich and complex view of what is necessary to encourage lifelong commitment to reading, and will be of interest to all those studying the nature of the reading process.

Hall, Christine, and Coles, Martin *Children's Reading Choices* 185pp. London and New York: Routledge ISBN: pbk 0 415 183887 1.

This book aims to answer the question of what children actually choose to read themselves and is based on a survey of nearly 8,000 ten, twelve and fourteen year olds in England, together with 87 supplementary interviews. The work builds on a previous seminal study by Frank Whitehead, *et al.,* in 1977. This publication therefore offers details of children's reading at a particular moment and also seeks to identify trends between the 1970s and 1990s. The influences of gender, class and ethnicity are considered. In summary, the book explores reading at different ages; favourite books and authors; the reading of magazines, newspapers and comics; differences between boys' and girls' reading; the influence of family background, including socio-economic background, ethnicity and family reading habits; children's own reading habits, including use of libraries and book ownership, and the use of multimedia. Recommendations and ideas of ways to judge quality in children's reading material are offered. There are numerous explanatory tables, and key references are given at the end of each chapter. Useful appendices provide the questionnaire and interview schedule used, together with project procedures and details of how different categories were chosen and coded.

Reference: Whitehead, Frank et al., (1977) *Children and their Books: the final report of the Schools Council Research Project on Children's Reading Habits, 10–15* London: Macmillan.

MacDonald, TH *The Road to Reading: A Practical Guide to Teaching your Child to Read* (1998) 309pp. London: Aurum Press ISBN 1 854 10 583 3. *Available from All Books for Children, Aurum Press Ltd., 25, Bedford Avenue, London, WC1B 3AT.*

This book is primarily addressed to parents who wish to teach their children to read at home. There is a chapter specifically dedicated to teachers and academics, however, that offers a rationale for the strategies described in the rest of this manual. The method suggested is based on the accumulated acquisition of phonic patterns and is a structured programme of reading and writing activities. Advice is given to parents on, for example, ways of explaining spelling patterns and their exceptions. The pedagogical style is almost scripted, with specific direction on what to say and what to point at in a text. Those who are looking for a strongly argued view in favour of phonics will find this book useful, as will parents who are concerned that their child is not learning at school.

Stainthorp, Rhona, and Hughes, Diana *Learning from Children who Read at an Early Age* 179pp. London and New York: Routledge. ISBN: hbk 0 415 17494 5 ISBN: pbk 0 415 17495 3.

Results from a three-year longitudinal research study of the reading progress of twenty-nine early readers from Reading, England are presented here. The work builds on earlier research by Margaret Clark, who studied precocious readers in Scotland (Clark, 1976). The authors investigated children's reading from before they started school to their first National Curriculum assessment in Y2 (when the children were aged seven). Set within the context of current knowledge about literacy development, full details of the research project are presented and the significance of the findings explored. Early positive experiences including sharing books with adults, observing people writing and exposure to environmental print were important to these early readers, alongside phonological sensitivity and alphabetic knowledge which enabled them to understand connections between spoken language and print. The authors suggest guidelines for teachers to use to help all children with their reading progress. The references and indeces will be helpful to those who wish to study this subject further.

Reference: Clark, Margaret (1976) *Young Fluent Readers* Oxford: Heinemann Educational.

Makgill, Jo *Guided Reading: Going Solo Under Instruction* Minibook 12, 36pp. Royston, Herts., UKRA United Kingdom Reading Association. ISBN: pbk 1 897638 18 3 *Available from: Unit 6, 1st Floor, The Maltings, Green Drift, Royston, Herts., SG8 5DB, UK.*

Guided Reading, part of the British government's Literacy Strategy in England, is an approach in which the teacher offers guidance to small groups of readers (and occasionally to individuals whose instructional reading level differs from the others in the class), helping them to access prior knowledge, make predications, process print and comprehend text. This short, comprehensive account of guided reading, written by a primary school English adviser in New Zealand, provides a clear description of this method and offers practical support, with suggested lesson structures and sample lessons giving consideration to beginning readers, early readers and fluent readers, and to fiction and non-fiction texts. There is a short bibliography. This publication will be of interest to teachers and parents who wish to learn more about current thinking on Guided Reading.

Oakhill, Jane and Beard, Roger (Eds.) *Reading Development and the Teaching of Reading* 238 pp. Oxford and Malden, Massachusetts: Blackwell Publishers. ISBN: hbk 0 631 20681 7. ISBN: pbk 0 631 20682 5.

The psychological research reported here offers insights into the acquisition and development of literacy and suggests implications for the teaching of reading. Several of the papers take issue with the New Literacy Studies' perspective and other views emphasising social and cultural contexts above psychological perspectives. The collection highlights instead: the importance of phonological skills; the links between orthography and phonology in English, alphabetic coding as a support for fluent reading; the importance of paying close attention to the words on a page and not being dependent on contextual cues to help word recognition; the connections between graphemes and phonemes activated during reading for meaning; the importance of spelling-to-sound relationships; early phonological awareness together with a use of the alphabetic principal (in contrast to an over-reliance on learned sight vocabulary), and evidence about phonological development and orthographic analogies. Leading authors in the field are represented, including Keith Stanovich, Charles Perfetti, Linnea Ehri, Usha Goswami, Connie Juel and Marilyn Jager Adams. Goswami's chapter also counters recent criticisms regarding an onset and rime approach to the teaching of reading. A scholarly work, this book, (which is based on a special issue of the *Journal of Research in Reading*, a UKRA journal), will be a useful resource for researchers, students and practitioners who wish to explore fundamental principles underpinning the teaching of reading.

Riley, Jeni *Teaching Reading at Key Stage 1 and Before* 188pp. Cheltenham: Stanley Thornes. ISBN: pbk 0 7487 3516 X. Available from Stanley Thornes Publishers Ltd., Ellenborough House, Wellington Street, Cheltenham, Gloucester, GL5 1YW.

This book is one of a series of titles aimed at ITT students and primary practitioners. It is a comprehensive guide to the teaching of reading in the early years, based firmly within the frameworks of the National Literacy Strategy and the National Curriculum for Initial Teacher Training (DfEE Circular 4/98) in the UK. The book provides a thorough introduction to key theories and relevant research in a number of areas including the reading process, the teaching of bilingual children and the role of children's books in the early years classroom. The author provides practical guidance throughout and uses illustrative case studies of children and classrooms in order to extend understanding and encourage further reflection. The book contains a range of structures which will be of help to readers including a statement of objectives at the beginning of each chapter, an ongoing glossary of technical terminology and summaries and pointers for further reading at the end of each chapter. This clearly written and up-to-date text provides a thorough introduction to the teaching of reading in the early years of primary schooling.

Roberts, Geoffrey R *Learning to Teach Reading* 120pp. London, Thousand Oaks: Paul Chapman, a SAGE Publications Company. ISBN: hbk 0 7619 6328 6. ISBN: pbk 0 7619 6329 4.

The second edition of this book now includes up-to-date information on the teaching of phonics, handwriting and literacy practices in the early years' classroom, supported by findings from research. It examines considerations to be borne in mind when thinking about children learning to read and offers a basic programme for teaching. It investigates the Literacy Hour in relation to a practically feasible and theoretically sound model of reading, and gives practical information about handwriting. Suggestions for further reading are included. This is a book that will be of interest to teachers and others working with children age three to ten.

Williams, Sara and Lewis, Tanya *Helping Young Children to Read in the Early Years* 152pp. London: Hodder and Stoughton. ISBN: pbk 0 340 73815 4. *Available from Hodder and Stoughton Educational, 338 Euston Road, London, NW1 3BH.*

This book is aimed at students on early years courses, but will also be of interest to teachers and parents. Essentially practical, the book deals with the development of reading from birth through to the early years of school. Starting with reading with babies and toddlers, there follows a chapter on the beginnings of reading, here subtitled 'pre-reading skills', challenges and special situations are addressed, reading at school and support outside school are explored, followed by ways to extend reading and fluency. Booklists and other resources are supplied together with brief information on assessment and the National Literacy Hour. The book is well presented, with clear photographs, quotations and children's drawings supporting the text. The authors are experienced at working with young children and their parents and in their communities.

Focus on Writing

Bolton, Gillie *The Therapeutic Potential of Creative Writing: Writing Myself* 252pp. London and Philadelphia: Jessica Kindersley. ISBN: pbk 1 85302 599 2.

This practical and thought-provoking book offers tried and tested methods of using writing therapeutically. Contextualised by the background and history of this approach, the book explores the potential healing nature of writing, keeping a journal, how to get started, using images, dreams, and writing poetry, fiction and autobiography. Writing in groups is explored within different contexts, including the doctors', hospital, hospice, prison and old people's home. The text is complemented throughout by illustrative examples of different types of writing. There is a list of useful contact addresses for those who wish to explore this field more fully, and an extensive bibliography.

Barnett, Robert, W and Blumner, Jacob, S (Eds.) *Writing Centers and Writing Across the Curriculum Programs: Building Interdisciplinary Partnerships* 222pp. Westport, Connecticut and London: Greenwood Press. ISBN: hbk 0 313 30699 0.

The contributors to this edited collection variously explore the relationship between Writing across the Curriculum (WAC) programmes and Writing Centers in a range of secondary and post-secondary institutions in the US. Each chapter describes a different situation in a different institution and examines how students' writing is taught and supported across the curriculum. The chapters show how writing policy decisions are made not just according to learning theories but are critically influenced by political circumstances in the institutions concerned. The locus of control for WAC varies across contexts: for example, in some institutions writing is taught in an integrated way within subject areas, while in others the English Department might retain the responsibility for the teaching of writing. The impacts of the various possible arrangements are explored across the chapters, with a consideration of the effectiveness of each permutation. The writers carefully convey a sense of the individual nature of each institution and its arrangements. The collection would provide a useful reference for all those interested in developing Writing Across the Curriculum policies in their own institution as well as those interested in literacy policy making and development.

Browne, Ann *Teaching Writing at Key Stage 1 and Before* 222pp. Cheltenham: Stanley Thornes. ISBN: pbk 0 7487 4041 4. *Available from Stanley Thornes Publishers Ltd., Ellenborough House, Wellington Street, Cheltenham, Gloucester, GL5 1YW.*

A thorough and well-presented overview of teaching writing for practising teachers and those in training, this book draws on current research findings on the development of children's literacy skills. The objectives each chapter aims to address are clearly stated, there are copious examples of children's work, activities for the reader to undertake, a summary at the end of each chapter, and further reading suggested. Key words are flagged in the margins, and the book also contains a helpful glossary of terms. The topics dealt with are: issues of writing in general; writing in school; organising writing; developing writing at different stages; spelling; handwriting; punctuation; writing in context; individual difference; assessing writing, and planning for writing. The book addresses the requirements of the National Literacy Strategy and the ITT National Curriculum. It would be helpful to use on courses of teacher training.

Edwards, Sylvia *Writing for All* 103pp. London: David Fulton. ISBN: pbk 1 85346 602 6. Available in North America from Taylor and Francis.

This book considers writing within the context of the National Literacy Strategy, now in its second year of implementation in the primary schools of the United Kingdom. Its aim is to support teachers in becoming more effective classroom practitioners and it describes itself as a 'practical manual' but all strategies are well contextualised within research-based academic argument. In addressing key issues, it defines 'effective writers'and offers strategies for differentiation, assessment and policy making. It looks in particular at raising standards in schools and at ways of addressing the difficulties different pupils may encounter.

Kellogg, Ronald *The Psychology of Writing* 253pp. Oxford: Oxford University Press ISBN: pbk 0 019 512908 3.

This book offers a cognitive psychological understanding of the process of writing. In his introduction the author identifies the area of writing as an omitted focus of study in cognitive psychology and here he seeks to redress the balance. Kellogg explores writing as a vehicle of thought and as a medium through which thought is expressed, developed and reified. Using meaning making as the primary lens through which the process of writing is explored, Kellogg identifies a range of writing and thinking types and analyses levels of difficulty amongst the identified writing types. He thus presents useful information to teachers and trainers as well as academics in the fields of literacy and cognitive psychology.

Kress, Gunther *Early Spelling: Between Convention and Creativity* 237pp. London and New York: Routledge. ISBN: hbk 0 415 18065 1. ISBN: pbk 0 415 18066 X.

'Spelling is one social convention amongst many' is a key message of this book, in which Kress challenges the current emphasis on correctness in the mechanical aspects of composition by asking readers to consider in detail a wide range of writing collected from children aged from 18 months to 12 years. In his closer, empathetic and serious analysis of these texts, he delves beneath surface features of spelling and drawing to find the complex thinking that lies behind what are often seen as errors, or as supplements to meaning, in children's work. He encourages teachers and researchers alike to understand the process of children's spelling, not as the reproduction of correct forms but as a means of acquiring a system of making meaning in which a wide range of semiotic resources can be deployed.

Qualifications and Curriculum Authority *Improving Writing at Key Stages Three and Four* 59pp. London: QCA. Reference No: QCA/99/ 392. *Available from QCA Publications, PO Box 235, Hayes, Middlesex UB3 1HF, UK.*

This booklet summarises the findings from a project commissioned by the Qualifications and Curriculum Authority, to investigate the accuracy and effectiveness of pupils' writing in relation to the official English Curriculum for England and Wales. Highly structured coding frames were used to identify specific linguistic features of texts produced by 16 year old pupils. Additionally, the analysts focused more generally on text structure, coherence and the establishment of reader-writer relationships. The ways in which these features contribute to the overall effectiveness of pupils' writing (in terms of examination criteria of the English National Curriculum) are identified. All those involved in teaching English in secondary schools, as well as their trainers, are the intended audience for this study.

Riley, Jeni and Reedy, David *Developing Writing for Difference Purposes* 191pp. London, Thousand Oaks: Paul Chapman, a SAGE Publications Company. ISBN: pbk 0 7619 6464 9.

The authors of this book begin with the premises that literacy is life enhancing; that writing complements reading; that the development of 'each language mode is inter-related'(page xii); that reading and writing develop thought and that writing is difficult. Riley and Reedy build on these propositions using a myriad of examples of children's work and argue strongly for the need to teach early years pupils the conventions of different genres. They demonstrate through detailed exemplification how teachers can provide frameworks of analysis for young readers and writers. This work shows clearly how knowledge about texts can be taught in a meaningful and practical way, alongside a whole range of reading and writing activities across the curriculum. The work is underpinned by a strong theoretical framework and would be useful to teachers, students, INSET co-ordinators and all those involved in early years literacy development.

Sassoon, Rosemary *Handwriting in the Twentieth Century* 208pp. London and New York: Routledge. ISBN: pbk 0 415 17882 7.

Aesthetically pleasing, with copious illustrations demonstrating different aspects of handwriting through the century, this book provides a thorough investigation of the history of how handwriting has been developed and taught, and in so doing offers a detailed historical record. Changes in educational policies, economic forces and the increasing sophistication of information technology have increased the predominance of speed and efficiency in the writing process, moving away from learning to write using copy books to a range of initiatives throughout the century. The work of key figures who have influenced the ways in which handwriting has been taught is explained and illustrated, and the impact of the National Curriculum in England and Wales is documented. The book takes an international perspective, and reports on handwriting around Europe and in America and Australia.

Focus on Language

Brent Language Services *Enriching Literacy – Text, Talk and Tales in Today's Classroom: a practical handbook for multilingual schools* 72pp. Stoke on Trent: Trentham Books. ISBN: pbk 1 85856 163 9. *In North America available from Stylus Publishing.*

Compiled by Robin Richardson from material developed on a range of INSET courses and projects organised by Brent Language Service in London, this text provides a series of well-grounded practical ways of working with pupils in bi-lingual classrooms. The diversity within bilingualism is illustrated through a series of pupil profiles; the richness and benefits of a multilingual background are demonstrated, as well as the challenges this cultural complexity represents for teachers. The book distinguishes between 'everyday language' and 'curriculum language', and demonstrates their respective roles. There are classroom examples of using writing frames, group talk and teaching key ideas though 'key visuals' (road signs; computer icons; photographs; charts and diagrams) and language patterns. The stories used in these culturally and linguistically mixed classrooms have universal themes, so promoting an inclusive learning environment.

Edwards, Sylvia *Speaking and Listening for All* 106pp. London: David Fulton. ISBN: pbk 1 85346 603 4. Available in North America from Taylor and Francis.

This text emphasises the relationship between language and learning and its primacy in human communication. It describes how all four strands within the English Curriculum – Reading, Writing, Speaking and Listening, interrelate. With an intended readership of practitioners and trainee teachers in the Primary sector in the UK, it refers in detail to the National Curriculum and the National Literacy Strategy, dealing with assessment, development and pedagogical issues. Practical ideas for ways of working with pupils in the classroom and for policy making are underpinned by theoretical argument and research-based techniques.

Lindfors, Judith Wells *Children's Inquiry: Using Language to Make Sense of the World* 274pp. New York: Teachers College Press and Urbana, IL: National Council of Teachers of English. ISBN: hbk 0 8077 3836 0. ISBN pbk 0 8077 3837 9. *Available in the UK through The Eurospan Group, 3, Henrietta Street, Covent Garden, London WC2E 8LU, UK.*

This book explores how children use language to learn about the world, themselves and each other. It shows how teachers can support (and inhibit) this process, using examples from a broad range of contexts. It uses the voices of both teachers and pupils to describe their learning and teaching experiences and contextualises their commentaries within the frame of Vygotskyan and Bakhtian theories of learning. Tangentially connected to literacy, this text would be useful to literacy academics and teachers seeking to explore the ramifications of concepts such as 'genre' in a broader linguistic framework. There are also extended references to classroom based literacy work (discussions about books and story writing sessions). While the focus of analysis is upon the spoken language, much is to be learned about the teaching of literacy from the discourse analyses, since they identify the literacy learning processes nurtured through discussion.

Pollock, Joy and Waller, Elisabeth *English Grammar and Teaching Strategies: Lifeline to Literacy* 102pp. London: David Fulton Publishers. ISBN: pbk 1 85346 638 7. Available in North America from Taylor and Francis.

The introduction to this book argues for the need to teach grammar in schools, on grounds that knowledge of grammar as essential for effective communication. It endorses the view that the acquisition of Standard English is crucial for social mobility and suggests that English people are now at risk of being 'outclassed in our own tongue'(page 3). This somewhat prescriptive opening is followed by a catalogue of grammatical terms with definitions and exercises for pupils designed to outline clearly the fundamentals of traditional grammar categories. A reference list for further reading is provided. This text could be a useful reference for teachers obliged to incorporate formal grammar work into their teaching as well as a workbook for pupils.

Qualifications and Curriculum Authority *Not Whether but How: Teaching Grammar in English at Key Stages 3 and 4* 67pp, Sudbury: QCA Publications. *Order Reference: QCA/99/418. Available from QCA Publications, PO Box 235, Hayes, Middlesex UB3 1HF, UK.*

This publication reflects the thinking and investigations of a working party under the auspices of QCA and provides a rationale and suggestions of approaches for the integration of grammar teaching within a content-related context of the English curriculum. Arguing strongly for the need for pupils to have explicit knowledge of grammar and the metalanguage to go with it, the book provides suggestions for ways of integrating grammar teaching within an existing curriculum. Intended to offer guidance to teachers who lack confidence in their own grammatical knowledge, or those who teach grammar as a strand separated from other work it offers a whole range of examples of how to comment on grammar in a variety of text types. It addresses problems associated with teaching grammar to less confident writers and to pupils for whom English is an additional language. While targeted at teachers in the UK using the National Curriculum for England and Wales, it would also be useful to teachers and teacher trainers working beyond this context.

Qualifications and Curriculum Authority *The Grammar Papers: Perspectives on the Teaching of Grammar in the National Curriculum* 60pp. London: QCA. Reference No: QCA/98/052. *Available from QCA Publications, PO Box 235, Hayes, Middlesex UB3 1HF, UK.*

Written because of concern about the teaching of grammar in schools as stipulated by the National Curriculum for England and Wales, this booklet describes ways in which the teaching of grammar can be meaningfully incorporated into the curriculum at Key Stages Two and Three. It advocates the explicit, systematic and consistent teaching of grammar and that it should include both oral and written work. Offering some explanation about the history of grammatical study, it moves into an exposition of the benefits of teaching grammar in contemporary classrooms. It describes, with examples, how the functions and meanings of grammatical structures can form part of other aspects of English teaching. Assessment of pupils' grammatical knowledge is also covered. In addition it reports the results of a survey into teachers' grammatical knowledge. Intended for teachers and student teachers in England and Wales, the booklet will also interest those seeking curriculum change as well as those looking for a useful history of attitudes to English grammar teaching.

BOOKS ON SPECIFIC ISSUES

Focus on Special Needs

Berger, Ann and Gross, Jean (Eds.) *Teaching the Literacy Hour in an Inclusive Classroom* 106pp. London: David Fulton Publishers. ISBN: pbk 1 85346 630 1. *Available in North America from Taylor and Francis.*

This book seeks to tackle the many reservations that might be expressed about a uniform literacy programme being applicable to all pupils. It begins by describing the in-built advantages of the Literacy Strategy in supporting the literacy learning of pupils with Special Educational Needs and offers answers to the anticipated problems teachers might experience in an inclusive classroom. It fully endorses the Literacy Hour as a modus operandi and provides a range of examples of differentiated work. The contributors to this volume represent a range of practitioners who have worked with the hour for two years and their suggestions are practical, based upon experience. Two case studies of teacher's work present highly optimistic accounts of the Hour, showing how pupils with Downs syndrome, hearing loss and behavioural problems for example, have been helped by the structured way of working. A final section on incorporating ICT brings the book fully up-to-date.

Berger, Ann, Henderson, Jean and Morris, Denise *Implementing the Literacy Hour for Pupils with Learning Difficulties* 117pp. London: David Fulton Publishers. ISBN: pbk 1 85346 615 8. *Available in North America from Taylor and Francis.*

The rationale behind this booklet is to apprise teachers who work with children with profound learning difficulties of methods of adapting the Literacy Hour to the needs of their pupils. It is convincingly argued that the Literacy Hour has much to recommend it for such pupils, but because of the general aim to include these pupils it is also in teachers' interest to become acquainted with the Hour.

It is intended for teachers who work in special or mainstream schools who have children with severe learning difficulties. Like other books in this series, this publication endorses the Hour and it shows how teachers can draw on a wide range of previously used teaching skills while implementing the Literacy Strategy. The most substantial part of this text provides two detailed Schemes of Work over three terms each, giving lists of activities, objectives and resources to be used.

Calver, Jane, Ranson, Sandy and Smith, Dorothy *Key Stage 2: Helping with Reading Difficulties* 66pp. Tamworth, Staffs: NASEN. ISBN: pbk 1 901485 05 6. *Available from NASEN House, 4/5 Amber Business Village, Amber Close, Amington, Tamworth, Staffs., B77 4RP, UK.*

Placing the teaching of children with reading difficulties in context, this publication begins by exploring processes of reading both as undergone by the pupils and within the text. The first part of the book looks at identification and assessment strategies. In part 2, different reading approaches are looked at in turn. Teaching reading through visual strategies, auditory strategies, contextual/ language strategies, and the motivational aspect are all addressed. Part 3 examines organisation in terms of the classroom, resources and of working with parents and other adults. References and useful addresses are included. Although the publication is intended principally for teachers working with children in Key Stage 2 of the National Curriculum, there is also helpful advice for teachers in other phases of education.

Department for Education and Employment *The National Literacy Strategy Additional Literary Support Module 1*. [Phonics and Spelling; Reading (Guided and Supported)] 111pp. London: DfEE ISBN: 0 19 3122252 7.

Department for Education and Employment *The National Literacy Strategy Additional Literary Support Module 2*. [Phonics and Spelling; Reading (Guided and Supported); Writing] 160pp. London: DfEE ISBN: 0 19 3122253 5.

Department for Education and Employment *The National Literacy Strategy Additional Literary Support Module 3*. [Phonics and Spelling; Reading (Guided and Supported); Writing (shared and supported)] 176pp. London: DfEE ISBN: 0 19 312224 3.

Department for Education and Employment *The National Literacy Strategy Additional Literary Support Module 4.* [Phonics and Spelling; Reading (Guided and Supported); Writing] 176pp. London: DfEE ISBN: 0 19 312225 1.

Department for Education and Employment *The National Literacy Strategy Additional Literary Support: Getting Started Preparation for the Teaching Programme* 95pp. London: DfEE ISBN: 0 19 312231 6.

All available from Department for Education and Employment, Sanctuary Buildings, Great Smith Street, London SW1 3BT.

These books comprise a package which resources the 'Additional Literacy Support Programme' (ALS), an integral part of the National Literacy Strategy used predominantly in English primary schools. The programme is intended to be used with pupils who have not been taught via the Literacy Hour throughout their primary school education. (The British Government's specified target for 80% of all eleven-year-olds is to reach National Curriculum Level 4 by the year 2002.) The programme has been specifically designed to overcome problems diagnosed by the Qualifications and Curriculum Authority as experienced by underachieving pupils in their Key Stage One tests (taken at the age of seven). Accordingly, each module focuses on specifically identified problem features. The modules describe teaching routines, provide word lists and OHTs, and promote the use of metalinguistic vocabulary with pupils (e.g. phoneme, split diagraph). A brief rationale is occasionally offered in the booklets, usually as part of the scripts to be used by teacher trainers, literacy co-ordinators and classroom assistants in the schools. Some of the linguistic terminology is explained. These books are specifically designed for teachers, trainers and classroom assistants who are teaching the National Literacy Strategy; the books are also of interest to literacy policy researchers.

Dockrell, Julie and Messer, David *Children's Language and Communication Difficulties: Understanding, Identification and Intervention* 192pp. London and New York: Cassell. ISBN: pbk 0 304 33658 0.

This book discusses how children who experience language and communication problems encounter difficulties in a whole spectrum of other areas of their lives. A spectrum of special needs is addressed, ranging from hearing and vision loss, to autism and learning disabilities. Within each special need identified, the impact of that need on a child's literacy development is discussed. The book identifies what specific provision is available for support, the developmental problems that children experience and the long-term impact of language disabilities. Those working with children with language and communication problems, student teachers, special needs support providers and INSET organisers would find this text useful.

Miles, TR, and Miles, Elaine *Dyslexia: A Hundred Years On* (Second Edition) 198pp. Buckingham and Philadelphia: Open University Press. ISBN: pbk 0 335 20034 6.

The aim of this book is to review the field of dyslexia over the past hundred years. This current edition is an extensively rewritten version of the original (published in 1990), taking account of advances in research and practice during the intervening years. In particular, chapters on dyslexia in different languages, beyond phonology, assessment and early diagnosis, counselling, and looking to the future have been extended and changed. Other chapters look at the origin of the concept of dyslexia, methods of investigation, phonological deficits, ocular and oculo-motor problems, brain research, genetics, and exploration of subtypes and remediation. Technical language has been kept to a minimum, making the book generally accessible, while extensive references allow readers to follow up in detail particular lines of enquiry.

Tod, Janet *Individual Education Plans: Dyslexia* 104pp. London: David Fulton. ISBN: pbk 1 85346 523 2. Available in North America from Taylor and Francis.

This book is designed to help Co-ordinators of Special Educational Needs produce Individual Education Plans for pupils who have been identified as dyslexic, in line with the 'Code of Practice' (DfE 1994) as used in England and Wales. The author provides examples of a range of ways in which the code has been interpreted and implemented successfully in different schools, to suit a range of pupil needs and school circumstances. In addition it shows how to integrate procedures for the development of Individual Education Plans within more general school development planning, illustrating ways of working with individual teachers to support the teaching of dyslexic pupils. The book thus offers guidelines to teachers who are not obliged to work within the UK system, for it provides fully rationalised strategies for supporting the acquisition of literacy skills in dyslexic youngsters. With its useful chapter about dyslexia itself, the controversies and concerns, the text will be of interest to teachers beyond the target audience in the UK.

Reference: DfE (1994) *Code of Practice on the Identification and Assessment of Special Educational Needs* London: HMSO.

Wilson, Angela *Language Knowledge for Primary Teachers: A Guide to Textual, Grammatical and Lexical Study* 166pp. London: David Fulton. ISBN: pbk 1 85346 606 9. Available in North America from Taylor and Francis.

This text is directed at teachers who need to, or wish to incorporate an element of teaching explicit knowledge about language in an integrated way with other aspects of literacy (and spoken language) work. It opens by explaining why teachers should incorporate Knowledge about Language into their work and demonstrating why it is that spotting features of language within text, such as similes, is often a redundant process lacking real meaning for children. The author spends some time describing features of different types of text and grammatical structures before moving onto describing how to use this knowledge in the primary classroom. This book will be useful to teachers and student teachers who wish to polish up their knowledge of grammar or are seeking imaginative ways of incorporating grammar teaching into their existing work.

Working Party of the Division of Educational Child Psychology of the British Psychological Society *Dyslexia, Literacy and Psychological assessment* 124pp. ISBN: pbk 1 85433 310 0. *Available from the British Psychological Society, St. Andrews House, 48, Princess Road East, Leicester LE1 7DR, UK.*

This report considers the concept of dyslexia and recognises the plight of learners who are diagnosed as dyslexic. The report evaluates the different theoretical explanations for dyslexia and suggests that these are not oppositional explanations but rather descriptions of different types of dyslexia. It is argued that quality of provision for dyslexic children in the National Literacy Strategy requires further research. The ways dyslexia is currently catered for and the effectiveness of current policy and practice are evaluated. A useful reference book for Educational Psychologists, Special Educational Needs Co-ordinators and all those involved in organising provision and training for the teaching of children with dyslexia.

Focus on Assessment

Barrentine, Shelby J (Ed.) *Reading Assessment: Principles and Practices for Elementary Teachers* 280pp. Newark, Delaware: International Reading Association. ISBN: pbk 0 87207 250 9. *Available from IRA, 800 Barksdale Road, PO Box 8139, Newark, DE 19714-8139, USA.*

Key articles from *The Reading Teacher,* an IRA journal published 8 times a year, are assembled together in this publication. The articles are grounded in research by leaders in the field and provide practical methods and ideas to implement assessment procedures. The emphasis is on integrating assessment with instruction, requiring new forms of assessment such as performance-based assessment, miscue analysis and portfolios. The book contains a list of additional readings in each section. This publication will be of help and interest to elementary teachers and those teaching and researching in Higher Education.

Brooks, Greg, Flanagan, Nicola, Henkhuzens, Zenta and Hutchinson, Dougal *What Works for Slow Readers? The Effectiveness of Early Intervention Schemes* (*Third impression, lightly revised*) 100pp. Slough: National Foundation for Educational Research. ISBN: pbk 0 7005 1480 5. *Available from NFER, The Mere, Upton Park, Slough, Berkshire, SL1 2DQ, UK.*

This study by NFER looks at the characteristics and effectiveness of twenty intervention schemes used in Britain with low attaining but non-dyslexic pupils. The book aims to make available clear and analytical information to teachers so that they can choose the best option for their students. Background information on the schemes covered and a flow chart to help find one's way through the various forms of intervention are provided in the first chapters. This is followed by a description and evaluation for each scheme, including parental involvement, Family Literacy, Paired Reading and Reading Recovery, to name only a few. References are supplied and an appendix with details of how the quantitative evaluations were carried out for each scheme is provided.

Sainsbury, Marian, Caspall, Louise, McDonald, Angus, Ravenscroft, Lesley and Schagen, Ian *Evaluation of the 1998 Summer Schools Programme: Full Report* 95pp. plus 4 appendices. Slough: National Foundation for Educational Research. ISBN: pbk 0 7005 1540 2. *Available from NFER, The Mere, Upton Park, Slough, Berkshire, SL1 2DQ, UK.*

This is a report of the second year of summer schools in England, when 50 hours of focused literacy tuition was provided for children aged eleven who were transferring from primary to secondary school (Key Stage 2 to Key Stage 3). A 10% sample of about 55 participating schools was examined. A pilot scheme of literacy for children with special educational needs was also evaluated, and here the target sample consisted of all summer schools (smaller pilot programmes for summer numeracy schools were also researched). Assessments of standards, attitude questionnaires and examination of target-setting provide the basis of the evaluation. The report is thorough and comprehensive, and sample breakdowns by background variables, text data, multi-level analysis for summer schools and questionnaire responses are provided in detailed appendices.

(Information on the training for this intervention can be found in Department for Education and Employment *The National Literacy Strategy Guidance for Providers of Summer Literacy Schools and Key Stage 3 Intervention Programmes for Literacy 1999-2000* 39pp. London: DfEE. described in the section on Literacy in the Secondary Years).

Focus on Family Literacy

Barone, Diane *Resilient Children: Stories of Poverty, Drug Exposure, and Literacy Development* 241 pp. Newark, Delaware: International Reading Association and National Reading Conference. ISBN: pbk 0 87207 199 5. *Available from the International Reading Association, 800 Barksdale Road, PO Box 1839, Newark, Delaware 19714-8139, USA.*

This is an exploration of the part literacy plays in the lives of children of drug addicted mothers through a study of 26 children, who were exposed to crack/cocaine parentally, with detailed case studies of six individuals' literacy learning at home and at school. The children in the study, all living in high poverty situations, proved to be interested in learning, and in most cases were performing at or above the expected level in literacy. The study is set in context and details of the methodology are provided. The implications of the study, both in general terms and for practice, are explored in a concluding chapter. The book clearly shows notable levels of resilience in children facing adverse circumstances. The text is supported by examples of the children's drawing and writing and there is an extensive bibliography. All concerned with the development of children's literacy will find this book of interest.

Blatchford, Roy (Ed.) *The RIF Family Guide to Encouraging Young Readers*, 218pp. London: Scholastic Children's Books. ISBN: pbk 0 590 63646 4.

Aimed at parents, this book from 'Reading is Fundamental, UK', offers dozens of very specific suggestions for reading-related activities which can be enjoyed with children at home. The activities are grouped under headings such as enlivening reading aloud, incentives and record keeping, cooking and recipes, shopping, car trips, newspapers, rainy-day ideas, television, seasons of the year, gifts, games and trivia, writing and visits to the library, zoo, museums, garden, playground and neighbourhood. The number and range of ideas is considerable, most originating from RIF volunteers in the United States (but here completely Anglicised). It is unlikely that any single individual or family could ever identify or devise so many activities. The book does not describe or reflect upon family literacy but provides a resource for extending it which may be appropriate for some families some of the time, if not for all families all of the time.

Lloyd, Trefor *Reading for the Future: Boys' and Fathers' Views on Reading* 47pp. London: Save the Children. ISBN: pbk 1 899120 94 7. *Available from: Publication Sales, Save the Children, 17, Grove Lane, London, SE5 8RD, UK.*

This booklet offers a summary of findings from interviews conducted with 52 boys aged four, seven and fourteen and 22 fathers, together with groups of parents and early years practitioners from under-five centres in London, set within the context of the current climate of interest in boys' reading and fathers' actual and potential involvement in their reading at school and home. The methods employed are described and include the questions from the semi-structured interviews. The main themes to emerge from the interviews are explored in relation to the boys, young men, fathers and early years prac-titioners, with plenty of quotations from the participants in their own words. Conclusions and implications for practice are outlined, and a short list of relevant references is given. This publication will be of interest to those involved in teaching reading, particularly at the early stages, and to parents. One of the outcomes of this work has been an interactive booklet for fathers (and other male carers), and sons:

Orme, David Read Me Another Dad! An activity book for fathers and their sons aged 3-5 16pp. London: Save the Children. ISBN: pbk 1 899120 99 8. Stories and activities are included together with suggestions of further resources and ideas.

Paratore, Jeanne R, Melzi, G and Krol-Sinclair, B *What Should We Expect of Family Literacy? Experiences of Latino Children Whose Parents Participate in an Intergenerational Literacy Project* 138pp. Newark, Delaware: International Reading Association and National Reading Conference. ISBN: pbk 0 87207 246 0. *Available from the International Reading Association, 800 Barksdale Road, PO Box 1839, Newark, Delaware 19714-8139, USA.*

Building on ten years' work, this book reports literacy research with Latino families and students, conducted in collaboration with teachers. It addresses the question of what we should expect of family literacy, by studying the effects of an Intergenerational Literacy Project. As outcome measures they explored inter-view and anecdotal data, report cards, attendance and retention data. Presented are methodology, profiles of the children, including detailed case studies of academically successful children, those who were making progress and those who were struggling in school; and analysis and interpretation of the results of the Project. They conclude that family literacy programmes, though making an important contribution to children's education, cannot on their own compensate for the problem of underachievement by Latino children. Appendices include instruments used for the data collection. The book will be of interest to researchers, policy makers and educators who are involved in family literacy and issues relating to English as a second or additional language.

Walton, Mike *Family Literacy and Learning* 64pp. Dunstable: Folens Publishers. ISBN: pbk 1 86202 489 8. *Available from: Albert House, Apex Business Centre, Boscombe Road, Dunstable, Beds. LU5 4RL, UK. (1998).*

This book uses material from an Education Extra/Roald Dahl Foundation Family Literacy project to indicate practical ways of involving the family in teaching literacy. The first chapter explores the context of such work and key issues. Literacy projects are described in two comprehensive schools; four primary schools plus one infant, two junior and one middle school; a high school together with a nearby primary and a community school, and outcomes from the different projects explored. Example materials are suggested including school policy statements, job descriptions, sample letters to parents and publicity material, course outlines, guidance sheets for parents, sample certificates and a list identifying key issues to consider. A list of useful contacts and short bibliography are included.

Focus on Libraries

Hay, L and Henri, J (Eds.) *The Net Effect: School Library Media Centers and the Internet* 308pp. Lanham: Scarecrow Press. ISBN: 0-8108-3601-7. *Available in the UK from Shelwing Ltd., 127, Sandygate Road, Folkestone, CT20 2BL.*

This is an edited collection of over forty chapters dealing with the changing needs of learning communities in the 'Information Age'. School library media specialists have been at the cutting edge in moves to incorporate technological developments into pedagogical approaches that provide learners with agency and independence. These chapters address a very varied range of issues concerning aspects of this process. The chapters were all papers presented at a Virtual Conference in 1997 by a range of international professionals working in information services. This results in a mixture of topics, grouped under ten headings: Censorship: More Problems, Possible Solutions?; Children's Literature and the Internet: Issues and Services; Critical Thinking in the Electronic Age; Electronic Collection Development: Selection and Management Issues; More Hot Spots for TLs; MOO* Trek: Using MOOs in Education; Multiple Personalities? Teacher Librarian, Cybrarian; Director of Information Services; Process and Product: How do We Assess Students' Work?; Professional Electronic Networks for TLs: The School Library Home Page. The book contains many URLs for WWW sites which are relevant to the topics addressed here and will provide a wealth of useful material for information specialists, school librarians and teachers who have responsibility for school libraries.

MOO = Multi User Domain (MUD) Object Orientation.

Reuben, Joan and Spiller, David *Paperbacks on Public Libraries LISU Occasional Paper no. 22* 58pp. Loughborough: Library and Information Statistics Unit (LISU), Loughborough University. ISBN: pbk 1 901786 16 1. Available from LISU, Loughborough University, Loughborough, Leicestershire, LE11 3TU, UK.

This detailed publication will be of interest to publishers, booksellers and library suppliers, as well as librarians and students and researchers with an interest in library usage. The survey details publication patterns, paperback provision in public libraries, views of users, and durability and cost effectiveness. User views indicate that more people preferred fiction to be in paperback form and non-fiction in hard-back. Reinforcement for durability was recommended. Research instruments used are given in appendices.

Spiller, David, Creaser, Claire, and Murphy, Alison *Libraries in the Workplace.* LISU Occasional Paper no. 20 226pp. Loughborough: Library and Information Statistics Unit (LISU), Loughborough University. ISBN: pbk 1 901786 13 7. *Available from LISU, Loughborough University, Loughborough, Leicestershire, LE11 3TU, UK.*

Commissioned by the British Library Research and Innovation Centre, this publication provides an overview of key issues and trends in workplace libraries. The research report presents findings from a questionnaire survey of ten library sectors in both commercial and non-commercial organisations. These were: government departments; non-departmental government organisations; voluntary agencies; professional, trade and learned associations; legal organisations; commercial and financial companies; energy organisation; pharmaceutical companies; management and information consultants, and food and drink manufacturers. Main findings are reported for each sector individually, followed by a comparison between sectors. Issues addressed include: the numbers of libraries and information centres in the organisation; whom they aimed to serve; how many people were targeted; how many of them used the service regularly; staffing issues; use of electronic resources; print resources; interlending; other services provided, and annual expenditure. Detailed information is provided through extensive figures and tables. The questionnaire used is provided in an appendix.

Spreadbury, Helen and Spiller, David *Survey of Secondary School Library Users. LISU Occasional Paper no. 21* 54pp. Loughborough: Library and Information Statistics Unit (LISU), Loughborough University. ISBN: pbk 1 901786 15 3. *Available from LISU, Loughborough University, Loughborough, Leicestershire, LE11 3TU, UK.*

This study investigates the role and use of school libraries in four London secondary schools, two in the state sector and two independent schools. Detailed findings are presented about the pupils' use of the library and their views of access and image. Staff and users are profiled, the connections between the curriculum and the library are explored, and the place of the school library in relation to recreational reading and information technology is addressed. The survey questionnaire used is supplied in an appendix. This study records change at a time when the way state schools are funded and the curriculum they deliver has altered, and when the role of information technology in learning, and libraries in particular, has burgeoned.

Timperley, Patrick and Spiller, David *The Impact of Non-Fiction Lending from Public Libraries. LISU Occasional Paper no. 2* 45pp. Loughborough: Library and Information Statistics Unit (LISU), Loughborough University. ISBN: pbk 1 901786 27 7. *Available from LISU, Loughborough University, Loughborough, Leicestershire, LE11 3TU, UK.*

This study investigated library users' borrowing of non-fiction books in three large libraries, through interviewing users as they returned the books they had borrowed. Details are given about the respondents, the books, user behaviour in choosing non-fiction, reasons for borrowing the titles (in relation to gender, age, site of library, and subject of books), the use of the books borrowed and their impact (investigating borrowing books for pleasure, hobbies, practical reasons, for a job, study, and personal learning), non-fiction borrowing and advocacy of public libraries, and non-fiction borrowing and stock management. Detailed tables and figures, references, details of survey sites, survey questionnaire and Public Lending Right subject categories are supplied.

Venturella, Karen, M *Poor People and Library Services* 190pp. Jefferson, North Carolina, and London: McFarland and Company. ISBN: pbk 0 7864 0563 5. (1998).

Community librarians and community educators who have been disheartened by cutbacks in library services will find much of interest in this collection of articles. Although written from a north American standpoint, it contains much of relevance to other countries. The book should also interest any teachers whose students include children and adults who live in rural or urban poverty. Subjects covered include poverty programmes for children, access to technology for low income groups and library programmes for the homeless. There are also chapters offering practical suggestions including advice on how to take effective action to improve access and a list of `poverty related organisations'. References and an index are provided for readers with an academic interest in the subject area.

REFERENCE BOOKS

Cartree, James (Ed.) *Talking Books* 266pp. London and New York: Routledge. ISBN: hbk. 0 415 19416 4. ISBN: pbk 0 415 19417 2.

This text offers fascinating insight into the work and lives of a range of children's authors. Each chapter concentrates on a separate author and provides answers to questions likely to be asked by children and their teachers about favourite authors. Biographical information, and the influence of other writers is offered in each case, details about how each author approaches the writing process and particular examples of the revision and drafting procedures are illustrated. All the authors have worked with pupils in schools and this aspect of their work is reflected upon too. In addition, indicative book lists are provided at the end of each chapter. This book would be an invaluable resource for teachers and librarians, but would also be relished by pupils seeking more details about their favourite authors.

Fountas, Irene, C and Pinnel Gay Su *Matching Books to Readers: Using Levelled Books in Guided Reading, K-3* 400pp. Portsmouth NH: Heinemann. ISBN: pbk 0 325 00193 6. *Available in the UK through The Eurospan Group, 3, Henrietta Street, Covent Garden, London WC2E 8LU, UK.*

A practical guide for teachers of reading, this publication offers a levelled book-list of thousands of children's books, appropriate from kindergarten to Grade 3, by title and level of difficulty, showing the number of words in each, the author and series and the publisher or distributor. Introductory chapters discuss matching books to readers, the role of levelled books within a literacy programme, creating a levelled collection, levelled collections in relation to reading systems, use within a guided reading programme, creating a classroom collection and a school book room, how to select quality books, acquiring books and writing grant proposals. Guided help is offered in using the book-list of nearly 300 pages. There is a short bibliography and subject index.

Nuba, Hannah, Sheiman, Deborah Lovitky and Searson, Michael (Eds.) *Children's Literature: Developing Good Readers* 191pp. New York and London: Garland Publishing. ISBN: hbk 0 8153 2395 6.

This American book is intended as a reference tool for teachers, parents, librarians and others concerned with providing appropriate reading material for children. The first section provides the context, dealing with the history of children's literature and how to assess quality children's books. The second part has an essay by an illustrator and a writer about their craft, and the third examines developing good readers, encouraging early readers, appropriate interactions with babies, literature for the preschool and primary grade years, making children's videos, and interactive children's literature. The final extensive section provides a listing of resources for children's literature in the US, including recommended books, details of book awards, magazines, clubs and relevant resource organisations.

Moon, Cliff *Individualised Reading* 39pp. Reading and Language Information Centre, University of Reading, Reading, UK. ISBN: pbk 0 7049 13453. *Available from Reading and Language Information Centre, University of Reading, Bulmershe Court, Earley, Reading RG6 1HY, UK.*

Updated annually, this 28th edition offers teachers information on how to grade books into 13 different readability levels, and covers the range of fiction, non-fiction and poetry books covered by the National Curriculum. The books, many with descriptors or annotations, are listed in order of difficulty. There is an index of all the publications mentioned and the stages to which they have been assigned. All have been tried and tested with children in school. New publications for this year are indicated.

Office for Standards in Education *The National Literacy Strategy: An Evaluation of the First Year of the National Literacy Strategy* 24pp. London: OFSTED. Reference Number: HMI 216. *Available from: OFSTED Publications Centre, PO Box 6927, London E3 3NZ, UK.*

This publication makes use of evidence from the inspection by Her Majesty's Inspectors (HMI) of literacy teaching and learning in the first year of the National Literacy Strategy (introduced by the UK government in the autumn term, 1998 to English primary schools). It also draws on material from inspections in the previous year, National Curriculum test results for English for children in years 2 and 6, and additional English tests, developed by the Qualifications and Curriculum Authority (QCA), taken by pupils in sample schools in years 3 to 5. Issues addressed include 'The quality of the teaching of the literacy hour', 'Leadership and management', and 'Training and support'. While the overall picture about the implementation of the Strategy is encouraging, particular concerns are expressed about teaching phonics and teaching writing.

Quinton, Kathryn (Ed.) Compiled by Zaghini, Edgardo *The Children's Book Handbook 1999* 60pp. London: Young Book Trust. ISBN: pbk 0 85353 478 0. *Available from: Young Book Trust, Book House, 45, East Hill, London SW18 2QZ, UK.*

This is a detailed and well presented guide to information about children's books, published annually, and considerably expanded for this edition. It is published by the **Young Book Trust**, a national charity working for and with those concerned with what children read. Information about the Trust is included. The UK section of the Handbook comprises information about: organisations concerned with children's books; Arts Boards and Councils; clubs, societies, magazines; publishers including those publishing or supplying dual-language books; dealers in second-hand and antiquarian books; literary and arts agents for children's writers and illustrators; book prizes; competitions and courses for children and for adults writing or illustrating for children; relevant courses; bestsellers and most borrowed books in 1998; guidelines for school book provision and events diary. The International section consists of: organisations concerned with children's books; magazines and journals; book prizes and events diary. The sections are clearly demarcated and there is a comprehensive index that makes the information easy to locate.

Reading Recovery National Network *Book Bands for Guided Reading* 142pp. London: Reading Recovery Network. ISBN: pbk 0 85473 564 X. *Available from: Reading Recovery Network, Institute of Education, University of London, 20, Bedford Way, London, WC1H OAL, UK.(1998).*

This booklet has been written to assist teachers to audit, organise and supplement reading materials at Key Stage 1 for guided reading. Three thousand texts are graded into one of ten bands which span working towards Level 1 to working towards Level 3. Reading Recovery levels are also given for each band. Advice on using the National Literacy Strategy framework is given and on teaching reading at Key Stage 1. An index of book titles in alphabetical order is provided so that the levels of individual titles can be checked.

Stones, Rosemary (Ed.) Compiled by Judith Elkin *A Multicultural Guide to Children's Books, 0-16+* 67pp. London: Books for Keeps. ISBN: pbk 1 871566 05 3. *Available from: Books for Keeps, 6. Brightfield Road, Lee, London, SE12 8QF, UK.*

An excellent compilation of useful information, thoughtfully organised. Details of the annotated books are arranged by category: board and early concept books; picture books; myths and legends; poetry and song; fiction, divided into age sections; information books, and organisations, publishers, supplier details and suggested further reading. Dual language texts and books available in a Big Book format are signalled. A collection of short relevant articles precede the book annotations. There is an author/title index for ease of reference. This publication will be helpful for teachers, parents, librarians and researchers with an interest in children's literature.

Stones, Rosemary (Ed.) *Children's Books about Bullying: A Books for Keeps Guide* 30pp. Reading: Books for Keeps and The Reading Language Information Centre, Reading ISBN: 1 871566 045. *Available from: Books for Keeps, 6. Brightfield Road, Lee, London, SE12 8QF, UK.*

This publication is more than a book list; the introduction justifies the need for a publication on books about bullying, presenting an argument about the persuasiveness of fiction and the need to tackle social issues through story. It traces the history of books about bullying and identifies the growing awareness of bullying in schools. It discusses how modern poetry has addressed bullying problems and lists books in order of age group, along with brief synopses. This booklet will be useful to librarians, teachers of PSE and English.

Author Index

Title Index